CHINA:

A Brief History

PROVINCES IN CHINA

HEILUNGKIANG

KIRIN

INNER
MONGOLIA

LIAONING

KANSU

HOPEH

SHANSI

SHANTUNG

NINGHSIA

KIANGSU

TSINGHAI

SHENSI

HONAN

ANHWEI

HUPEH

CHEKIANG

SZECHWAN

KIANGSI

HUNAN

FUKIEN

KWEICHOW

TAIWAN

YUNNAN

KWANGSI

KWANGTUNG

CHINA:
A Brief History

SECOND EDITION

Nancy Faust Sizer

Phillips Academy
Andover
Massachusetts

Drawings by
Rebecca Rudd Sizer

Longman
New York & London

Grateful acknowledgement is made to the following for permission to reprint excerpts from copyrighted material:

To Harper and Row, Publishers, Inc. for Pearl S. Buck, *The Good Earth.* Copyright 1931, 1949 by Pearl S. Buck. Copyright renewed 1958 by Pearl S. Buck.

To Charles Scribner's Sons for Robert Van Gulik, *The Lacquer Screen.*

To Houghton Mifflin Company, for E. Backhouse and J.O.P. Bland, *Annals and Memoirs of the Court of Peking.*

To Harvard University Press, for T'eng and Fairbank, *China's Response to the West,* copyright (c) 1954 by the President and Fellows of Harvard College.

To G. P. Putnam's Sons for Roger Pelissier, *The Awakening of China 1793-1949,* copyright (c) 1966 by Martin Secker & Warburg Limited and G. P. Putnam's Sons.

To Columbia University Press for Wm. Theodore deBary, *Sources of Chinese Tradition.*

To Doubleday and Company, Inc., for Langdon Warner, *The Long Old Road in China.* Copyright 1925, 1926; and for Pa Chin, *Family,* copyright (c) 1972.

To Macmillan Publishing Co., Inc., for James E. Sheridan, *China in Disintegration: the Republican Era in Chinese History 1912-1949.*

To William Morrow & Company for Theodore H. White and Annalee Jacoby, *Thunder Out of China,* copyright 1946 by William Sloane Associates, Inc.; renewed 1974 by Theodore H. White and Annalee Jacoby.

To Robert Payne for his *Mao Tse-tung: Ruler of Red China.*

To International Publishers for quotation from the writing of Mao Tse-tung.

To Grove Press, Inc., for Edgar Snow, *Red Star Over China;* copyright (c) 1938, 1944 by Random House, Inc.; copyright (c) 1968 by Edgar Snow.

To Putnam's - Coward, McCann & Geoghegan, Inc., - Marek for Bao Ruo-wang (Jean Pasqualini) and Rudolph Chelminski, *Prisoner of Mao.*

To Random House, Inc., for "China Youth Daily" from Franz Schurmann and Orville Schell, *Communist China,* Vol. 3 of "The China Reader."

To New York Times Books for its *Report from Red China.*

ISBN 0-88334-119-0   91908988
                      4567890

For Ted
and for our children
Tod, Judy, Hal and Lyde

CONTENTS

PREFACE

It seems to many the ultimate in exotica to be teaching Chinese history to American adolescents. The author well remembers the elderly lady who asked, "What do you teach at Andover?" To the reply, "China," she responded, "Do you find that you can get the boys and girls interested in Wedgwood these days?" In spite of such minor discouragement, however, nothing was going to stop me from teaching Chinese history. It had been my conviction for years that young Americans would be fascinated by China's heroes, its villains, the Chinese preoccupation with moral issues and by the efforts of so many to cultivate a high standard of humanity against a backdrop of poverty. Yet from the first the difficulty of finding a good text plagued me. Although there are some good books on China, they were either too detailed, abstract, or too simplistic, and, if a collection of readings, too limited for readers who are new to the field. We Asian history teachers are often alone in our departments, usually teaching European or American history as well, and thus we don't have the chance to prepare elaborate curricula from scratch.

The book was developed to meet my problems as a teacher at Andover, at Cambridge High and Latin School and at Bradford College. In it, an effort has been made to include a little of everything needed both by teacher and student. The essays are mainly historical narrative, with an emphasis on the political events which underlie the course of history. In the documents are personal descriptions, sometimes of political figures, but also showing what Chinese society was like in different eras. Through the use of maps, poetry and even lists, I have tried to add more information in a relatively painless fashion. And finally, through the drawings of my friend and colleague (and as of June 1980, my daughter-in-law!) Rebecca Rudd Sizer, students can get a sense of the visual richness of China, and of the interest and integrity in so many of her faces.

The book is designed for writing as well as for reading. Notes can be taken from its essays, and the documents were chosen for purposes of contrast. More personal views put a different perspective on the essay, reflecting both an objective and a subjective approach. These subjects may be discussed, or they may be written about, or both, depending on the kind of time a teacher has, or how much writing he or she feels it is important for young historians to do.

Responsibility for whatever is in this book is of course assumed by the author, yet I have been helped by many. My former teachers Edward V. Gulick of Wellesley College and John K. Fairbank of Harvard University have read the manuscript and have offered me suggestions on it, as have Donald B. Cole of Phillips Exeter Academy, Frederick S. Allis, Jr., Chairman of the History Department at Phillips Academy, and my husband, Theodore R. Sizer, its Headmaster. Most of all, I am grateful to Ted and our children for their belief in me and their support of my work.

Nancy Faust Sizer

Major Dates and Persons in Modern Chinese History

Pre-modern History:
 551-479 B.C.: the life of Confucius
 200 B.C. - 1644 A.D.: China's great traditional dynasties, including the Han, T'ang, Sung, and Ming

Modern History:
 1644-1912: the Ch'ing (Manchu) dynasty
 1661-1722: the reign of the K'ang-Hsi Emperor
 1736-1795: the reign of the Ch'ien-Lung Emperor
 1793: Lord Macartney's Mission from Great Britain to China
 1839-1841: the Opium War, started after Commissioner Lin Tse-hsu tried to cut down the opium trade
 1842: the first of China's "unequal treaties": The Treaty of Nanking
 Late 1840's until early 1860's: The Taiping Rebellion, under the leadership of Hung Hsiu-ch'uan
 1851-1861: the reign of the Hsien-feng Emperor
 1861-1908: the dominance of Tzu Hsi, the Empress Dowager
 1860's: the "Self-Strengthening Movement," engineered at first by Tseng Kuo-fan, later by Li Hung-chang
 1870: The Tientsin Massacre
 1895: The Sino-Japanese War, ended by the Treaty of Shimonoseki
 1896-1899: the extension of foreign "spheres of influence" throughout China
 1898: The One Hundred Days of Reform, attempted by the Kuang-hsu Emperor
 1900: The Boxer Rebellion, followed by the Boxer Protocol
 1911: The "Double-Ten" Revolution against the Manchu throne
 1912: The formation of a Chinese Republic, at first under the leadership of Sun Yat-sen
 1912-1916: Yuan Shih-k'ai leader of China
 1912: the founding of the Kuo Min Tang by Sung Chiao-jen
 1913: Sung Chiao-jen assassinated
 1916-1926: the warlord period
 1919: The May Fourth Movement
 1921: the founding of the Chinese Communist Party by Ch'en Tu-hsiu
 1923: the alliance between the Kuo Min Tang, the Chinese Communist Party and the Comintern

1926: the Northern Expedition of the KMT and the CCP, led by Chiang K'ai-shek

1927: the "Nanking-Wuhan split" in the KMT, after which the Communists and the Kuo Min Tang openly opposed each other

1930-1934: the Ching Kang Shan period for the Communists, with the rise of Mao Tse-tung to power

1931: the "Mukden Incident" and Japan's takeover of Manchuria

1932: Chou En-lai's move from Shanghai to Ching Kang Shan, where he settled for a position beneath Mao's in the leadership hierarchy

1934-1935: The Communists' Long March, followed by the Yenan Period

1936: the "Sian Incident," after which a "United Front" was arranged between the KMT and the CCP in order to fight the Japanese

1937: the "Incident at the Marco Polo Bridge" and Japan's subsequent takeover of eastern China

1937-1945: China's war against Japan

1938: the removal of the government to Chungking, in Szechwan

1946-1949: the Chinese Civil War between the KMT and the CCP

1949: "Liberation" - the CCP in charge of all of mainland China

1950-1953: the Korean War

1951-1952: the Three-Anti and Five-Anti campaigns

1953-1957: the First Five Year Plan

1956: the Hundred Flowers campaign

1958-1961: the Great Leap Forward

1965-1968: the Great Cultural Revolution

1971: the Lin Piao Incident

1972: President Nixon's trip to China, the beginning of "normalization" between the U.S. and China

1976: the deaths of Chou En-lai and Mao Tse-tung; Hua Kuo-feng the leader of China

1976: the discrediting of the Gang of Four

1977: Teng Hsiao-p'ing restored to power

1977: the beginning of a modernization campaign

1978: U.S. recognition of Communist China announced by President Carter

MAJOR CITIES IN CHINA

• MUKDEN

• PEKING

TIENTSIN •

PORT
ARTHUR

• SIAN

NANKING •

• SHANGHAI

WUHAN
•

CHUNGKING

• CHANGSHA

CANTON

• HONG KONG

XIII

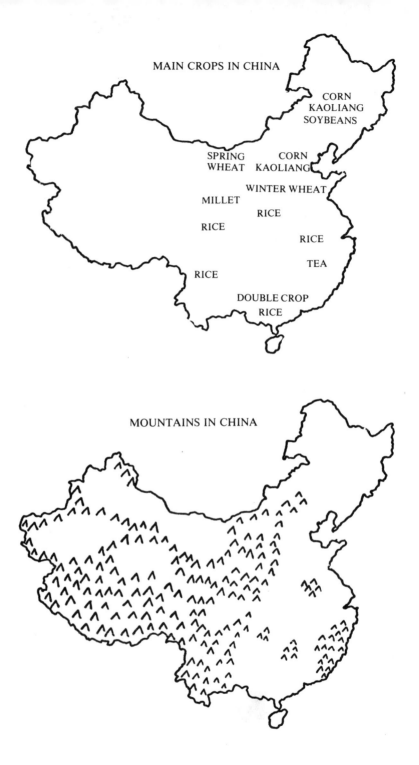

MAIN CROPS IN CHINA

CORN
KAOLIANG
SOYBEANS

SPRING   CORN
WHEAT   KAOLIANG

WINTER WHEAT

MILLET
        RICE
RICE
            RICE

            TEA

RICE

DOUBLE CROP
    RICE

MOUNTAINS IN CHINA

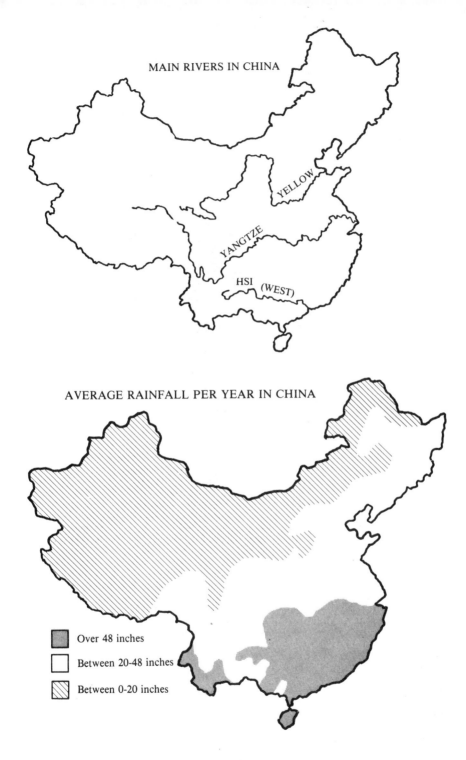

MAIN RIVERS IN CHINA

YELLOW

YANGTZE

HSI (WEST)

AVERAGE RAINFALL PER YEAR IN CHINA

Over 48 inches

Between 20-48 inches

Between 0-20 inches

XV

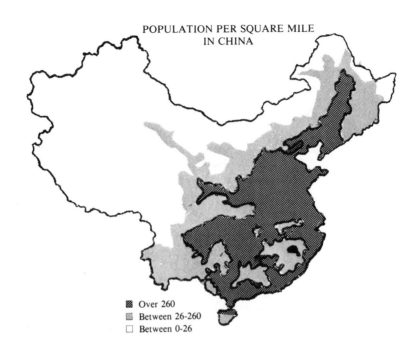

POPULATION PER SQUARE MILE
IN CHINA

▨ Over 260
▥ Between 26-260
☐ Between 0-26

1

Confucius and the Chinese Family

In China, governing has traditionally been done by the family rather than the state. Even before the time of Confucius, about 500 B.C., and certainly once his teachings were accepted as the main philosophy of most Chinese, it was the family, rather than the individual, village, or nation, which represented the most powerful, prestigious and responsible social grouping. Confucius was born into a world of chaos and poverty; even then there was a feeling that it was the family which could be the most fundamental source of security, and at the same time indicate rules of individual conduct and responsibility.

Even in Confucius' time, ancestor worship existed. It was based on the idea that any person who now lived would never have been born if it were not for his ancestors. It was his ancestors who kept the line unbroken, perhaps at considerable sacrifice. They had lived decently, successfully, attending to the ritual worship of the gods and to the land. Now it was one's own turn to keep the family line going, mindful of the standards and hopes of the past as well as those of the future.

Confucius understood and embraced those feelings, and it was he and his brilliant disciple Mencius, who lived about two hundred years later, who put these values into the words which have been studied and treasured by the Chinese for thousands of years. Confucius felt that one learns about the world by engaging in important relationships which start in the family, existing perhaps between a child and his father, or maybe two children of different ages. With maturity comes marriage, and a new and important relationship, that between man and wife. As one grows more aware of society outside the family, a subject will have a relationship with his ruler, the Emperor, or perhaps with the ruler's emissary. It will be very similar to the one which he had with his father. And, finally, there is the relationship between friends.

In every relationship, except possibly at times that between friends, there was unequal status. There was always a more powerful person who exerted authority, protection and generosity over

1

and on behalf of another. A young person growing up in this elaborate system of contacts, security and restraint picked up his cues from the important people around him as to what life was and would be like. From his father and his older brother he would learn not only what could and could not be done, but also, by observation, what role he might play in the family some day. Beyond that, he would learn that with power over others comes considerable responsibility for their welfare. Making this awesome discovery (which often had been pointed out by his mother), would serve to keep him "in his place" until he was well along in years.

The essence of contact between persons, for Confucius and for his millions of followers, was in this relationship, this predictable role-playing. One learned one's place in relation to others, even adjusting language, such as the words used to describe people; all depended on the status of the person being addressed. With those who were older, a humble attitude was usually adopted; toward those who were younger, a protective role would likely be assumed.

Just as age and place in the family assured a certain status, so did sex. Confucius believed that women were naturally inferior to men. Although a man might feel partnership in certain areas of family life, he would feel superiority in others. As time went on, the woman's place in Chinese society grew even more tenuous. In the upper classes, the men often took concubines, who acted as second wives, respected in the household, although never quite replacing the first wife. When a man died, his widow was not expected to remarry.

The biggest indication of the woman's inferior position in Chinese society was the custom of footbinding. In an effort to keep their feet small and dainty — and thus attractive to men, who attached great importance to it — young women actually sacrificed their ability to walk. Wrapping their feet tightly with cloth strips from the time they were seven or eight years old, they persisted — or their mothers persisted, in spite of the cries of the children — until their arches were actually broken, and their feet looked like upside down "lilies." Thereafter, although their feet grew numb and thus less painful, they were constantly subject to infection, and the young women could get around only in a kind of totter; but their mothers purportedly knew best, and the daughters, after all, did find husbands.

Although in its earliest days, in Sung times, footbinding was limited to the upper classes (those who could afford to keep their wives and daughters idle), it gradually spread to nearly all the women in China. One exception were the Hakkas, an unassimilated minority group which had migrated from the north to settle in groups in western and southern China. They were small merchants, and the women helped in the stores, undoubtedly aided by the steadiness of their normal feet. For the rest of China, however, effiency was sacrificed to beauty, and to the convenience of marriage for a woman.

The Bride and Groom Kneel Before Their Parents as part of the Ritual of the Wedding

Marriage for a woman meant that she would go to live in her husband's house or perhaps that of his parents, and, except for short visits or disasters, she would from that time on be cut off from her own family. She could then begin childbearing, and when a son appeared, his mother would be considered a real adult. A young woman raised in her own family to be lighthearted and perhaps even strong-willed would probably find herself unappreciated in the family into which she married. She would then hasten to adapt, to become quieter, more self-effacing and helpful, and in this way please her mother-in-law, who was often quite dictatorial within her own sphere. If she were the wife of an eldest son, her prestige in the family would grow as his did, and she might well become dictatorial, at least in the area of family management, by the time she had daughters-in-law of her own.

In the same way, a young man's place in the family would probably shape his personality. The oldest son, included in more and more conversations with his father and uncles, would become more serious and much more adult than his younger brothers. His father's treatment of him would be firm, authoritarian, but in time would come to include respect and even comradeship. Toward his younger sons, daughters and daughters-in-law, the head of the family would feel charity and responsibility, but no feeling of having to explain his actions. His sense of accountability was to the Chinese family system rather than to them as persons.

Indeed, inequality was thought of as a "good." As Mencius put it: "There must be those who are gentlemen and those who are countrymen. Without the gentlemen there would be none to rule the countrymen; without the countrymen there would be none to feed the gentlemen." Although they were not equals, people were attached to each other; for Confucians, this attachment was reciprocity, the stuff of which families were made.

Family life, furthermore, was all-encompassing in China. Over the centuries, many families were poor and small and even a bit disorganized. But the ideal was a large and stable family called a "clan," and close relationships within the family extended over generations and often into remote degrees of kinship. Cousins were expected to be as close as brothers would be in other cultures. Often they lived in the same compound group of houses connected around a central courtyard, or at least in the same neighborhood.

Land was held by families rather than by individuals, and the many activities centered around working the land were undertaken in common. Some eighty-five per cent of the Chinese people were thus employed, and family ties were reinforced. Many of the activities which in other cultures are supported by hired strangers — babysitting, care for the aged, family entertainment, insurance, health care, fire protection — all were handled within the family or clan unit. Even religious ritual was undertaken primarily in common; many families had set up their own shrines, indoors and out. All such activities tended to make a person feel more like a family member rather than an individual or a member of a larger society. When a member felt touched and bound by the concerns of the family, Confucians thought, he then achieved his highest moral development as a person, and society as a whole was at its most safe and strong.

There were, of course, problems with this system. At times the power held by certain family members was not tempered with mercy and good judgment. Although the tales of female infanticide in China have been exaggerated, there was a good deal of child slavery. Such a system, an intricate web of relationships, depends for its strength on stability. If a clan member has to spend thirty years in steady, loyal apprenticeship, he must be secure in the knowledge that he will eventually have a chance to enjoy greater status. If not that, then he must at least be able to count on security and on being fed. Chinese literature and history give many examples of these disappointments, based, not on anger at the system per se, but on failed expectations within it.

Yet on the whole, for most of China's recorded history, legitimate expectations were met, and, for hundreds of years, China provided a stable, if not affluent, society. The family, by helping to fashion and temper individual expectations, did much to help provide this stable society. The maintenance of order, one of the main purposes of any society, was handled almost entirely by the family. Walls were built around the compounds and care was taken to guard against not only thieves coming in from the outside, but also thieves going out from their own family ranks. This was not out of pure altruism on their parts; they knew that they would all be considered responsible, and thus punished, for the deeds of an errant family member. So they disciplined themselves.

At several different points in Chinese history the system of pao chia, or "linked security," was instituted. A number of families would join together to protect themselves against fire, flood, famine, and especially bandits. The enemy was not only outside the compound, but those in the pao chia would watch each other carefully as well. This grouping and its sense of joint reponsibility was certainly one of the most important forerunners of communalism — or even communism — in China, and it came directly out of the development of the Chinese family.

Besides the pao chia system, local gentry families helped to keep order in their areas. Certain families, holding more land than others, also held more responsibility. They would arrange the planting and landworking schedules, at least for the land they controlled, and would influence others. They served as mediators in most arguments which came up, and arranged for many of the local religious rituals. They were also advisors to local government officials, if any were nearby, but if there weren't, the gentry essentially ran things.

The Chinese family, handling so many problems for itself, was introverted and self-sufficient, and this led to another of its defects. Constant subordination of one's own needs to those of the family — for example in arranged marriages, which were more often based on family than on personal needs — often robbed a person of the opportunity for emotional or intellectual self-development. To have spent the afternoon reading a good book, or talking with a close friend, might have seemed very selfish.

Even the job of keeping so many relationships in working order was energy-absorbing for the average Chinese person, and left him little opportunity for extrafamily thoughts or pursuits. Budding inventors, organizers or radicals, if not appreciated in their own clan, had little chance to go elsewhere. This in itself down-played the value of their contribution, and invention, reform and scientific discovery were not admired or encouraged in much of traditional China. Closing the circle, an institution which depended on stability helped to keep China all the more stable, even static.

The old family system lasted until the early part of the twentieth century, becoming threatened at the same time as the ideas of Confucius on which it was largely based. When young Chinese people began to admire the West, not only for its inventions and industrial development, but also for the prosperity and the relative air of freedom within most western families, they began to chafe against, and finally to abandon, the idea that families can only be built around role-playing between unequals in a threatening and unchanging society.

In traditional China, however, the family perfectly complemented the state, and it did much of the work which modern states, including modern China, feel they must undertake. Since the imperial government apparatus was light, it was, for all its pomp and majesty, relatively inexpensive. And that is how the Chinese people, for many long centuries, seemed to want it to be.

A Collection of Confucian Analects

Tzu Kung asked: "Is there any one word that can serve as a principle for the conduct of life?" Confucius said: "Perhaps the word 'reciprocity': Do not do unto others what you would not want others to do to you."

Confucius said: "The humane man, desiring to be established himself, seeks to establish others; desiring himself to succeed, he helps others to succeed. To judge others by what one knows of oneself is the method of achieving humanity."

"Let the prince be as a prince. Let the minister be as a minister. Let the father be as a father. Let the son be as a son."

Tzu Fu asked about filial piety. Confucius said: "Nowadays a filial son is just a man who keeps his parents in food. But even dogs or horses are given food. If there is no feeling of reverence, wherein lies the difference?"

"If a man's natural qualities exceed his training he is uncultivated: if his training exceeds his natural qualities he is little more than an educated lackey. It is only when the natural qualities and the training harmoniously complement each other that we have the gentleman."

Confucius said: "Lead the people by laws and regulate them by penalties, and the people will try to keep out of jail, but will have no sense of shame. Lead the people by virtue and restrain them by rules of decorum, and the people will have a sense of shame, and moreover will become good."

Chi K'ang Tzu asked Confucius about government, saying: "Suppose I were to kill the lawless for the good of the law-abiding, how would that do?" Confucius answered: "Sir, why should it be necessary to employ capital punishment in your government? Just so you genuinely desire the good, the people will be good. The virtue of the gentleman may be compared to the wind and that of the commoner to the weeds. The weeds under the force of the wind cannot but bend."

The Duke of She asked about good government. Confucius said: "A government is good when those near are happy and those far off are attracted."

Confucius said: "Learning without thinking is labor lost; thinking without learning is perilous."

"At one point during Confucius' travels, he was so poor that he

was hungry. When asked by an angry disciple whether it was fit-
ting that a gentleman should endure such things, Confucius
replied, 'It is only the gentleman who is able to stand firm in the
face of hardship; the ordinary man, finding himself in want, is
swept off his feet.'

"What do you say?" Tzu-kung asked, "of a man who is liked by
all of his fellow citizens?" "That is not enough," the Master told
him. "Then what about one who is disliked by all of them?" "That
is still not enough to judge from. The best thing would be for them
to be liked by the good, and disliked by the bad."

Confucius said: "At fifteen, I set my heart on learning. At thirty,
I was firmly established. At forty, I had no more doubts. At fifty, I
knew the will of Heaven. At sixty, I was ready to listen to it. At
seventy, I could follow my heart's desire without transgressing what
was right."

The Birth of a Son

The old man looked up from his bowl to say,
"Eat, or all will be cold." And then he said, "Do not trouble yourself yet – it will be a long time. I remember well when the first was born to me it was dawn before it was over. Ah me, to think that out of all the children I begot and your mother bore, one after the other – a score or so – I forget – only you have lived! You see why a woman must bear and bear." And then he said again, as though he had just thought of it newly, "By this time tomorrow I may be grandfather to a man child!" He began to laugh suddenly and he stopped his eating and sat chuckling for a long time in the dusk of the room.

But Wang Lung stood listening at the door to those heavy animal pants. A smell of hot blood came through the crack, a sickening smell that frightened him. The panting of the woman within became quick and loud, like whispered screams, but she made no sound aloud. When he could bear no more and was about to break into the room, a thin, fierce cry came out and he forgot everything.

"Is it a man?" he cried importunately, forgetting the woman. The thin cry burst out again, wiry, insistent. "Is it a man?" he cried again, "tell me at least this – is it a man?"

And the voice of the woman answered as faintly as an echo, "A man!"

He went and sat down at the table then. How quick it had all been! The food was long cold and the old man was asleep on his bench, but how quick it had all been! He shook the old man's shoulder.

"It is a man child!" he called triumphantly. "You are grandfather and I am father!"

The old man woke suddenly and began to laugh as he had been laughing when he fell asleep.

"Yes - yes - of course," he cackled, "grandfather - grandfather -" and he rose and went to his bed, still laughing.

Wang Lung took up the bowl of cold rice and began to eat. He was very hungry all at once and he could not get the food into his mouth quickly enough. In the room he could hear the woman dragging herself about and the cry of the child was incessant and piercing.

"I suppose we shall have no more peace in this house now," he said to himself proudly.

When he had eaten all that he wished he went to the door again and she called to him to come in and he went in. The odor of spilt blood still hung hot upon the air, but there was no trace of it except in the wooden tub. But into this she had poured water and had pushed it under the bed so that he could hardly see it. The red candle was lit and she was lying neatly covered upon the bed. Beside her, wrapped in a pair of his old trousers, as the custom was in this part, lay his son.

He went up and for the moment there were no words in his mouth. His heart crowded up into his breast and he leaned over the child to look at it. It had a round wrinkled face that looked very dark and upon its head the hair was long and damp and black. It had ceased crying and lay with its eyes tightly shut.

He looked at his wife and she looked back at him. Her hair was still wet with her agony and her narrow eyes were sunken. Beyond this, she was as she always was. But to him she was touching, lying there. His heart rushed out to these two and he said, not knowing what else there was that could be said,

"Tomorrow I will go into the city and buy a pound of red sugar and stir it into boiling water for you to drink."

And then looking at the child again, this burst forth from him suddenly as though he had just thought of it, "We shall have to buy a good basketful of eggs and dye them all red for the village. Thus will everyone know I have a son!"

The next day after the child was born the woman rose as usual and prepared food for them but she did not go into the harvest fields with Wang Lung, and so he worked alone until after the noon hour. Then he dressed himself in his blue gown and went into the town. He went to the market and bought fifty eggs, not new laid, but still well enough and costing a penny for one, and he bought red paper to boil in the water with them to make them red. Then with the eggs in his basket he went to the sweet shop, and there he bought a pound and a little more of red sugar and saw it wrapped carefully into its brown paper, and under the straw string which held it the sugar dealer slipped a strip of red paper, smiling as he did so.

"It is for the mother of a new-born child perhaps?"

"A first-born son," said Wang Lung proudly.

"Ah, good fortune," answered the man carelessly, his eye on a well-dressed customer who had just come in.

This he had said many times to others, even every day to someone, but to Wang Lung it seemed special and he was pleased with the man's courtesy and he bowed and bowed again as he went from the shop. It seemed to him as he walked into the sharp sunshine of the dusty street that there was never a man so filled with good fortune as he.

He thought of this at first with joy and then with a pang of fear. It did not do in this life to be too fortunate. The air and the earth were filled with malignant spirits who could not endure the happiness of mortals, especially of such as are poor. He turned abruptly into the candlemaker's shop, who sold incense also, and there he bought four sticks of incense, one for each person in his house, and with these four sticks he went into the small temple of the gods of the earth, and he thrust them into the cold ashes of the incense he had placed there before, he and his wife together. He watched the four sticks well lit and then went homeward, comforted. These two small, protective figures, sitting staidly under their small roof – what a power they had!

2

Government in
Traditional China

As we have seen in Chapter One, most of the job of order-keeping in China was done for hundreds of years by the large and substantial gentry families in the countryside. There was thus no need for an elaborate and expensive central government. Nevertheless, there were a few enterprises which were traditionally handled by the central government, often with great success. Around these functions grew up the notion of the Chinese Empire.

The first of these functions concerned defense, primarily of the northern Chinese farmers from the nomads of the inner Asian steppes. There had never been a time in recorded Chinese history when the northwestern direction had not been considered a menacing one. The nomads' forays, usually on horseback, were brief but destructive; they snatched food, weapons, even women, and then they fled, to leave a legacy of both impoverishment and fear. Against the nomads had been built several walls, roughly from southwest to northeast, and these were finally connected by the First Emperor of the Ch'in dynasty, in the third century before Christ, to become The Great Wall. It was an effective barrier to horses, and gave the defenders valuable time, as long as it was repaired often enough and manned by reliable soldiers. Construction, maintenance, and expansion of the frontier on the north and west thus became the earliest and one of the most important tasks of the central government.

Other tasks were those of building and then regularly dredging the Grand Canal, so that taxes in the form of rice could be brought to the capital, which was usually at Peking; dredging and building dikes against the Yellow River, "China's Sorrow," known for the loess soil which it carried, which was destructive during floods, yet a fertile remainder once the waters had receded. The central government also saw to the building and management of the Imperial City; the sponsorship of history writing, or of the various arts; the maintaining of religious and state rituals; the sending off of missions to other countries, or, more often, the receiving of missions from abroad. The government collected taxes, sometimes

The Great Wall

in rice or grains, sometimes in money and labor. It supervised the government monopoly over all salt mined or sold, and of course it had the constant job of organizing the Empire, and of securing the right people to run it.

As the organization of the Empire became complex, with a pyramid of officials at the capital, provincial, and finally down to the county (hsien) level, the Emperor in Peking grew worried that the government itself might be getting conservative or self-protective. Thus he established a censorate, or an arm of government responsible only to him, whose job it was to check on the rest of the government to make sure that all was being done as they claimed. If it was not, they had to report on specific failures. Censors were trusted by no one, except the Emperor, and they had to be very brave fellows, especially in certain treacherous times when even their Emperors occasionally turned against them.

When one considers how splendid was this Empire, how much care was taken over its structure and integrity, how impressive it seemed to its neighbors and even to westerners, and how sophisticated it was in its Confucian assumptions about the nature of man and how he can be helped to become his best self, one of the most surprising aspects of this Empire is how few its functions were, and how few personnel there were, relative to the population of China, in its Imperial government.

At the head of the government was the Emperor, almost inevitably a male, gaining the throne by a combination of heredity and suitability from within the ruling dynasty. He was primarily a symbol of both the authority and the compassion of the ruling family. He was called the "Son of Heaven," and held what was believed to be a "Mandate of Heaven" — in other words, a kind of permission of Heaven to rule over the people and function as intermediary between heaven and earth. His family had, it is true, gained power for their dynasty primarily by beating all of their competitors. This might have meant simply that they were the strongest, not necessarily the best. Nevertheless, it was considered that the people's faith in the leader's ability to become a good ruler had also contributed to his victory, both because their faith in him was sensed by "Heaven," which determined such things as luck and circumstances, and because of the people's own well-timed activity or passivity. As the saying put it: "Heaven sees as the people see; Heaven hears as the people hear."

This linking of Heaven's intentions with earthly power is not unusual in human history. Western rulers, too, have at times been considered to rule by divine right, and the Japanese feel that their royal family is descended in an unbroken line from the Sun Goddess herself. But in China the acknowledgment that power corrupts and that families can fall on hard times is built right into the theory: the Mandate stays constant, but the leaders receiving it are always subject to removal.

In the West we tend to think of past history in one line, fluctuating but basically headed in one direction, that direction called Progress. The idea that a nation's leadership could cycle, that a government could start over every 200 or 300 years, seems strange to us. But dynastic cycles fit in with the idea that ruling families come into power because they are considered good men, and they lose power when the people no longer believe them to be good as men or leaders. Thus the "command ethic," or the idea that the powerful should prevail, is coordinated with but succeeded by the "virtue ethic," the idea that the good are naturally going to gain power, will wield it effectively because they are good and can persuade others, and are going to lose it when they are no longer perceived to be good and have therefore lost their powers of persuasion.

The typical pattern was this: a strong leader and his small group of supporters won the Mandate and set up their dynasty. They had plans for the welfare of the people, expensive plans, but, because their group was small, the proportion of visible gains as compared to expense was still quite large. Their first job was usually one of tax reform: making it more consistent, plugging the loopholes, which had the effect of distributing the taxes more evenly among the people. As years went by the rulers were raising taxes, but at the same time accomplishing large and impressive projects, such as canals and dikes, expansion of the frontiers, or artistic flowering. In this early period their own power was not in danger, and did not need to be shored up or paid much attention.

Later in the dynasty, however, the Emperor and his advisors faced a proliferation of family, in-laws, supporters, retainers, and those who were owed favors of one kind or another. Lands were taken off the tax rolls as different families joined the gentry. This meant everyone else had to pay more to cover the rising expenses. A greater distance grew between rich and poor, and there was more bitterness. Enemies arose, which meant that time and money had to be devoted to the leader's own protection. Time, flattery, intrigue, weariness caused the dynasty members to take power and luxury for granted, forgetting that there was once a time when such conditions did not exist.

The court's eunuchs, men who were castrated so that they could be trusted to protect the Emperors' wives and concubines, came to have a too preponderant and often sinister influence. Expenses went up, vigor and vigilance went down, and the gap between what was offered and what was paid for grew embarrassingly large. Magistrates were not watched as carefully, the Censors grew afraid to speak the truth, and examinations were not conducted with as much integrity.

In this chaos there grew up the only form of dissent which could occur in China: the secret society. Since opposition to the ruler seemed unnatural to the Chinese — as the saying put it, "One Sun in Heaven; one ruler on earth" — there was no opportunity for open disagreement or a minority political faction. During hard times, there was inevitably a growth, both in numbers of societies and of members, of these restless, cohesive, and often antidynastic groups. By forcing opposition to go underground, the Chinese government made it more radical and violent. It was more difficult to know about, and certainly to control.

Sooner or later, the dikes were not repaired, which led to floods; or the canals were not dredged, which led to famines; or the frontier was not secured, which led to barbarian invasions. These were agonizing for the people, and were considered to be Heaven's "signs" that the Imperial family had lost its goodness, its concern for them, and therefore its right to rule. The leaders had ceased to be moral examples, which was the clear Confucian prerequisite for power. And so the people, following both their own inclination and what they perceived as Heaven's will, rose up in rebellion to support one of many contenders (usually backed by a secret society), who declared that the Emperor had lost the mandate, and the cycle started again. Typically, a dynasty lasted about two hundred to three hundred years.

There were variations to this pattern, but it is in this way that the great Chinese dynasties, the Han and the T'ang, the Sung and the Ming, as well as the last dynasty, the Manchu or Ch'ing dynasty, spent their courses.

It is Ch'ing dynasty which will concern us most in these pages. Besides existing from 1644 until 1912 and thus clearly part of modern Chinese history, it is full of fascinating contrasts. It offers examples both of the traditional outlook and of the pull toward modernization. A foreign dynasty, originating in Manchuria, north of the Great Wall, it ruled China by gaining the support of the Chinese gentry, and it was this dynasty which defended the Chinese in their first large-scale confrontations with the western world. The Manchus, clearly impressed by Chinese culture and determined to master it, nevertheless felt that the way to survive as the rulers of China was to preserve their own identity. They kept to themselves socially, refused to intermarry with the Chinese, to wear Chinese costumes or to allow their women to bind their feet as the Chinese women did. Young Manchu leaders knew Chinese well, but they were not allowed to forget the Manchu language. Young Chinese leaders of great promise were asked to learn Manchu. Along with their awe of the Chinese literary and scholarly tradition, the Manchus clearly felt a sense of superiority toward the Chinese, similar to that which a rough but brave frontiersman would feel toward the well educated or the sophisticated.

The Manchus gave China two of the best Emperors which it has ever had, which helped to establish the dynasty early. The K'ang Hsi Emperor, who ruled from 1661, when he was seven, until

1722, was a composite of all the best qualities which a Chinese Emperor could possibly have, with a few prized Manchu traits thrown in.. He was first of all a compassionate ruler, interested in his people, famous for the trips which he made among them, even to the far away and hostile south, in order to get to know them better. He was interested even in the details of government, inspecting dikes himself and learning as much as he could about their upkeep, but insisting also on frugality and efficiency in government. In this way, he established himself as a ruler who cared about whether the people were getting enough to eat, thus following advice of Mencius, who linked morality and human welfare when he said, "If beans and millet were as plentiful as fire and water, there would not be such a thing as a bad man among the people."

A hunter and warrior, K'ang Hsi kept his body fit and his mind alert with trips which he took periodically to the hunting areas of Manchuria. He was a well-trained scholar even by Chinese literati standards, and he won their support, not only for his own erudition, but for his support of the arts, extensive dictionary work, and the writing of history. He himself produced a group of moral maxims called the Sacred Edict, which is reproduced in the documents section of this chapter. It was a collection of advice on the best way for Chinese to conduct themselves, with an eye to both their own consciences and their reputations among their neighbors. The Sacred Edict, drawn largely from Chinese sources, especially Confucianism, was read aloud by the local governmental figure every two weeks to the assembled populace; therefore it must have been known well by every Chinese person.

K'ang-Hsi's grandson, the Ch'ien Lung Emperor, was also a figure of consequence, long reign (1736-1795), energy and literary production. His reign is often considered to be the high point of Manchu success in China. By the end of his reign, when he was becoming senile, he had a few favorites who used their power unwisely, and the decline of the dynasty had begun.

The Manchus, who followed the Chinese lead in government in so many respects, did add one unique feature. They created a system of dual posts, held by both a Manchu and a Chinese appointed together to do one high-level job. Each was to have his own contribution to make, but their rivalry on the spot was also considered to be good for the Empire. The sharing of responsibility was Confucian, reminding one of the pao chia, but it also showed the special nature of foreign rule in China. This pattern is also significant because it has been revived by the Communists, who frequently appointed both "Reds" and "Experts" to share positions in the late 1960's.

These Chinese members of the government deserve a more extended description, since it was they who manned the Empire, dynasty after dynasty, and frequently they who determined whether a dynasty succeeded or failed. The best way to learn about the life and work of these officials would be to create an imaginary figure, for example a Wang Chih, whose experiences would be typical, and then follow him throughout his career.

Portrait of a Scholar Bureaucrat

Wang Chih was born into a gentry family. He was their first son, and clever even from childhood. Like most gentry families, Wang's was looking for just such a child because they were eager to have connections within the scholar bureaucracy which ran China. Therefore, even when he was young, there were tutors hired for him, and his schoolwork grew increasingly serious every year. If Wang had not been from a substantial family, his chances for an education would of course have been limited. In certain areas, however, there were schools set up for intelligent boys of more modest means, there being no class qualifications for becoming literate. Thus a poor boy, such as Confucius himself had been, could join the bureaucracy, in theory and even occasionally in practice.

Wang's education revolved around reading the Confucian classics: the analects of Confucius himself, the ancient works which came before Confucius and were believed to have influenced him, and the commentaries on Confucius by Mencius and other favored disciples such as the Sung scholar, Chu Hsi. Given a phrase or sentence, Wang Chih was able after a few years of study to identify its source, explain its meaning, and write what was called an "eight-legged-essay" on the basis of the fragment which he had been given. His essay would consider the idea presented from eight points of view, include a few pertinent literary allusions, and emphasize balance, style, even calligraphy more than imagination or depth. This kind of expertise required a good memory, an elegant and economical writing style, and a willingness to follow the lead of the examiners in what constituted scholarship.

Wang Chih turned out to be good at all of these skills, and willing to follow the regimen of the typical exam schedule. He therefore sat for the first level of the exams, in a nearby town, and he did well enough to be accepted to the second level of examinations, which would be held the next year in his province's main city. Some of his fellow students were not successful, but they prepared themselves to take the examinations again and again until they could pass them. Of course, there were always many who were never successful, and Chinese ghost stories are full of "failed scholars" who wandered around the countryside in a desolate and half-crazed state, yet somehow extremely attractive to women. Many of these unsuccessful candidates could find some sort of work which built on their literacy, and they enjoyed a higher status than others (for example, once literate, they could not be publicly flogged), but they could not join the government officially unless their families could buy one of the small percentage of posts which were reserved for that purpose.

Our successful candidate, Wang, after a year of solid study, travelled to the provincial capital, where he passed the examination at the second level, and then finally to the third level exam in Peking. The government took great care in both of these levels to make sure that the exams were conducted without favoritism or any breach of integrity. Each candidate was given a little cubicle in which to write, so that he would never be able to look over anyone else's shoulder, and he signed his name with a number, known only to the one who kept the master list. This would ensure that the readers would respond only to the work done, and not to the name or reputation of the scholar. When he finally, after years of study, of travel, and of waiting for examinations, passed the third level of examinations, he had won the coveted "chin-shih" status, was called a "presented scholar," and it was the Emperor himself to whom he would be presented, and who would often conduct his own oral examination.

Only then was Wang able to become an official, and he had to wait in Peking until there was a post for him. Like most others of the new scholar bureaucrats, his first post was to be the Magistrate of the lowest level of governmental organization, the hsien. There were between 1000 and 1500 of these units during the Ch'ing dynasty. If he had written a particularly brilliant examination, the best seen in years, he might have been sent to the provincial level, or even kept in the capital. But Wang was mindful of how severe the competition was, and he was grateful for his appointment.

His family, who loved him and who had subsidized this whole process, might have hoped that Wang Chih would be sent home to become an official in his home town, where he could indeed have been very helpful to them. But the rules of the Empire precluded just that handy possibility with a "law of avoidance," which insisted that the scholar bureaucrat be sent to provinces different from his own. He was also switched from post to post in different provinces, usually about once every three years. This was specifically designed, as were so many other aspects of the appointment process, to hold him to a manner of utmost integrity, impartiality, and concern for the needs of the many rather than of the few.

However noble this process was in its design, however appropriate a measure to counter China's reverence for the family rather than the state, the "law of avoidance" was very hard for Wang to live with, and it may have led to the very result which the government feared. When Wang arrived at his first post, he found that he would be the Magistrate, or the chief government figure, in a hsien of about 250,000 people, which consisted of one walled town, a few large and many small villages. An optimist by nature and an idealist after so many years of exposure to Confucianism, Wang expected that although there were many people for whose lives he was responsible, he could somehow learn about them, and communicate with them, effectively and quickly. After all, he had always been a smart and strong person.

But Wang soon learned that he couldn't understand the local dialect — not at all! Of course, he could communicate with those local people who were literate, a tiny percentage, because Chinese characters were the same all over the nation. A few of the gentry, too, might be able to speak in the Mandarin dialect, which Wang had learned in Peking. But in China there were so many dialects, and they differed so much one from another, that the average person might be completely unable to understand someone who lived only twenty miles away. Thus Wang found himself isolated from the very people whose needs he was supposed to understand, and to learn about them, even to do anything for them, he had to depend substantially on the clerks and runners who worked in his yamen, or office.

Good judgment, no matter how earnestly it is cultivated, depends on the information which one gets. These yamen workers did not feel bound by the Confucian humanitarian ethic; they had not travelled up the examination ladder; nor were they governed by the "law of avoidance." Although great care was taken that they come from a good family — defined as one not engaged in one of the "mean" professions, such as merchandising or banking — the clerks were a difficult group of people for the Magistrate to try to control. Given power, they could not resist its abuse. They knew things about the district and the office that he could never learn quickly enough. Thus, as time went on, Wang found that it was the clerks, and not he himself, who were setting the tone in the yamen, facing the public daily, deciding what should be done, and, especially important in China, deciding the manner in which it would be done.

Besides being cut off from the real business of the hsien by his inability to know its people personally, Wang found himself more and more absorbed in paperwork. The number of documents required by his office and of letters which had to be written to his superiors was immense; and each one had to be put together carefully, so that its meaning would not be misunderstood or tampered with as it travelled from his office to all those which stood between him and Peking. In addition, Wang's own promotions would be awarded on the basis of the style, clarity and form of those letters, documents, and other examinations which Wang would take, as well as the peace and prosperity of his hsien, and his delivery of the proper amount of taxes. Of course, it was assumed that Wang would be an impressive and honorable public figure, read the Sacred Edicts well, carry on the other rituals of the office with dignity, and dress and behave as a Magistrate should. If he did all these things, Wang hoped, he could inspire all who worked in the yamen to benefit by his example as a Confucian gentleman.

Wang's education cannot be said to have been of great use to him as he was setting up the administration of his first hsien. Although he could certainly remember everything that Confucius had said on any subject, there were problems which came up two thousand years later which could not conceivably be handled by following an analect. Nor were there general guidelines to follow; the Chinese avoided them, on the theory that "when a state is about to perish, the regulations increase in number." Instead there were literally hundreds of procedures, often confusing and contradictory. If a local situation perplexed him, he could always write a letter to his superior, but these letters had to be impeccable in form and calligraphy, both coming and going, and the mails were slow, so that the situation might well have resolved itself, or blown into a harmful crisis, by the time the reply was received.

When a dynasty was running well, the Censorate provided a way for a Magistrate to find out whether he was doing well and to have a colleague with whom to talk over governmental matters. At other times, however, Censors were timid, incompetent, or petty tyrannizers.

Although he tried hard, Wang was not able to achieve all that he set out to do. There was a great deal of corruption in the yamen, and there had been for years. Wages were either nonexistent or else so low for the yamen workers that it was assumed that they would have to supplement their incomes by accepting bribes, called "customary fees," for every different kind of service; these fees were, as one disgusted official put it, "as numerous as the hairs on an ox."* Besides the fees, the clerks and runners often got money through extortion, bribery, and manipulation of the tax collections. After a while, a "likin" tax was developed on products which were moved from place to place, providing a good bonus for the clerks. The government, forced by Peking to levy taxes even in times of local distress, and offering very few services which could be seen by the local people, soon came to lose its compassionate image. The Magistrate was supposed to be the local "wise man," able to help his people to sort out their troubles. Like other Confucian leaders, such as the head of a family, he ruled by relationship. In fact, the Chinese people did not turn to him or his office for mediation, preferring to arrange their compromises elsewhere, in their guilds or with the help of their local gentry. They were probably wise to do this, for he couldn't know them well, and besides, Chinese justice was expensive, erratic and could at times be very cruel; there was a general feeling that anyone so cantankerous as to have to use the courts would deserve whatever judgment was dealt out to him. As the document from the Judge Dee mystery shows, the Magistrate's office was a combination of impressive benevolence and outright terror, often existing side by side, yet each seemingly unaware of the other's existence.

Wang was troubled by this, but he soon learned that he would not get ahead if he developed a reputation as a complainer or a hothead. After two more tours as a Magistrate, he was promoted to be Governor of a province. Now he had to deal with the Magistrates below him as well as with Peking, and although he sympathized with their entreaties to send help to their areas, either in the form of tax relief or public works help, he had to try to see the Empire as a whole, with all of its demands, instead of just one small part. This gave him an air of impartiality, a quality he was quite proud of, but he wondered sometimes what had happened to the fierceness with which he had once attacked the problems of the poor farmers in his district. He worried to see his sensitivity and perhaps compassion going, but he had other things on his mind. First of all, his own career was by no means secure: promotions

*Ch'u Tung-tsu, *Local Government in China under the Ch'ing,* (Cambridge, Massachusetts, 1960), p. 49.

A Scholar Bureaucrat with his Wife and Concubine

were getting harder and harder to win, and his own salary was also quite low considering his expenses, so that he felt he had to figure out ways to add to his income without actually taking part directly in what had come to be called "the squeeze." Usually his solution for this was simply to raise taxes which presumably would be sent to Peking, but then subtract his own share from those taxes on their way through his office. Of course, if enough others did that as well, there would not be much left for Peking! The central authorities might protest, investigate thoroughly, send Censors to make sure Wang and his fellow scholar bureaucrats were doing their jobs properly; or perhaps Wang would be able to get away with it. He had to take the chance, but he tried to keep the slippage of money down to a minimum.

Wang's feelings of responsibility for the Empire came, not so much out of a pride at personal honesty or achievement, but from his desire to be part of a smoothly working social unit. He saw his function as the setting up of a system of connections and mutual responsibility between people. He helped it along, but in an unobtrusive way. He did not presume to be an imaginative or charismatic leader, and his constant moving from post to post kept him from being very well-known or popular in any one area.

Under a system of mutual responsibility, a man is guilty of any crime or indiscretion committed by one with whom he is closely connected. Thus if a person stole, his parents, his children or his employer would be considered responsible for the restitution of the property if the thief himself could not be found. The job of the Magistrate was not so much to determine who was guilty as it was to supervise the process of returning to social harmony. The pattern must be restored. He would decide what acts of retribution on the part of the responsible would restore peace to the community or honor or property to the aggrieved.

Wang never had a promotion beyond that of Governor. The dynasty was declining during the latter days of Wang's career, and so he never knew whether it was because of inertia, or that his minor corruption was suspected, or that his district's problems were held against him in spite of his efforts. At any rate, he was able to help his brothers and cousins in various ways, and he built himself a comfortable living in his last years in the government. Any extra money he used to buy land of his own, which he considered the only safe and honorable investment for a man of reputation and family. He always enjoyed reading the Classics and devising little essays around them, and he looked well in his Mandarin's robes even when he was seventy.

Thus it was a combination of the following different elements which, all together, carried out the functions of government in traditional China: the Emperor in Peking, the scholar bureaucrats in their posts all over China, the yamen workers who to varying degrees carried out the Magistrate's instructions, and finally, the local gentry, who were connected with the Empire more through a similarity of outlook and a sharing of responsibility than through more formal ties.

The Sacred Edict (K'ang-hsi Emperor, 1670)

1. Pay just regard to filial and fraternal duties, in order to give due importance to the relations of life.
2. Respect kindred in order to display the excellence of harmony.
3. Let concord abound among those who dwell in the same neighborhood, thereby preventing litigations.
4. Give the chief place to husbandry and the culture of the mulberry, that adequate supplies of food and raiment be secured.
5. Esteem economy, that money be not lavishly wasted.
6. Magnify academical learning, in order to direct the scholar's progress.
7. Degrade strange religions, in order to exalt the orthodox doctrines.
8. Explain the laws, in order to warn the ignorant and obstinate.
9. Illustrate the principles of a polite and yielding carriage, in order to improve manners.
10. Attend to the essential employments, in order to give unvarying determination to the will of the people.
11. Instruct the youth, in order to restrain them from evil.
12. Suppress all false accusing, in order to secure protection to the innocent.
13. Warn those who hide deserters, that they may not be involved in their downfall.
14. Complete the paying of taxes, in order to prevent frequent urging.
15. Unite the pao and the chia, in order to extirpate robbery and theft.
16. Settle animosities, that lives may be duly valued.

A Scholar Bureaucrat's Rationale: Poem Attributed to Tu Fu

It is not that I lack the desire to live beside rivers and among
    hills,
Hearing the wind scatter leaves, watching the rain breed fish;
But the thought of disproportion in public affairs
Offends my sense of rhythm, and disposes me
To expend the passion that normally takes form in song and
    painting
On matters of administrative interest.
Knowing that all things have their intrinsic nature,
I, being the breed of the dragon, imitate the whale
That perpetually aspires to change the currents of the sea.
Torn by contradictory thoughts, I drink deep.

A Magistrate's Court

"Magistrate, you are on a holiday!" Chiao Tai said reproachfully.

"Yes, I am!" Judge Dee said with a bleak smile. "But I must confess that I would like to see a bit more of my colleague Teng, without him knowing it. Further, I have presided over a tribunal so often that I would like to see the proceedings from the other side of the bench, for once. It'll be an instructive experience, for you also, my friend! On our way!"

The two men made slow progress, for it had grown a little cooler, and a dense crowd was about. But when they crossed the open square in front of the tribunal compound, they saw no one near the gatehouse. Apparently the session had started already and the spectators were assembled in the court hall. They passed underneath the stone archway of the gatehouse, where hung the huge bronze gong that announced the beginning of each court session. The four guards sitting on the bench eyed them indifferently.

They hurriedly ran across the empty main courtyard and entered the shadowy hall. From far in the back they heard a monotonous voice droning a lengthy statement. The two men remained standing just inside the door, letting their eyes adjust themselves to the half darkness. Over the heads of the crowd of spectators standing together farther down, they saw against the back wall the high bench, covered with scarlet cloth, standing on a raised dais. Behind it was enthroned Magistrate Teng, resplendent in his official robe of shimmering green brocade, and wearing the black judge's cap, its two stiffened wings standing out on either side of his head. He seemed engrossed in the document in front of him, slowly tugging at his goatee. Counsellor Pan stood by the side of his chair, his hands folded in his sleeves. The magistrate's bench was flanked by two lower tables where the court clerks were sitting. Behind the one on the right stood a grey-haired man, evidently the senior scribe, reading aloud a legal document. The entire back wall of the hall was covered by a dark-violet screen-curtain. In its centre the large image of a unicorn, the symbol of perspicacity, was beautifully embroidered in gold thread.

Judge Dee went on and joined the crowd of spectators. Raising himself on tiptoe he could see four constables standing in front of the bench, carrying iron chains, clubs, hand screws and the other

27

terrifying paraphernalia of their office. Their headman, a squat brutish-looking man with a thin ringbeard, stood somewhat apart, fingering a heavy whip. As usual everything in the tribunal was calculated to impress the public with the majesty of the law, and the awful consequences of getting involved with it. Everyone appearing there, old and young, rich and poor, and no matter whether complainant or accused, had to kneel on the bare stone floor in front of the bench, shouted at by the constables and, if the magistrate ordered so, cruelly beaten on the spot. For the fundamental rule of justice was that everyone appearing before the bench was considered guilty until he was able to prove his innocence.

Robert Van Gulik, *The Lacquer Screen,* (Charles Scribner's Sons, New York) pp. 22-24.

3

The Foreign "Devils"

While China was engaged in the massive job of running one of the largest empires on earth through benevolence and rationality, it was understandably absorbed in itself. The Confucian outlook does not encourage adventurousness of spirit, which explains the relative standstill both of scientific inquiry and of foreign exploration. Of course, there were exceptions, such as the inventions of wheelbarrow, crossbow, and kite, and also the naval expeditions, reaching as far west as Africa, sent out by the Ming dynasty during the fifteenth century. These exceptions were impressive as isolated achievements, but not as an expression of consistent interest in the new and unexplained. Westerners think that it is enough to justify their interest in something by saying that they want to know more about it "because it's there." In China there would have to be a better reason than *that*. Most of the real brains and energy in China went into the consideration of human relationships, and of how human experiences could be fitted into the world order.

While not looking outward, the Chinese nevertheless accepted other persons, goods and even ideas into their own country. One of the most important of these transplants was Buddhism. It was a religion based on the teachings of Gautama Buddha, an Indian, in 500 B.C., who believed that since life was essentially painful, the best thing a person could do would be slowly and self-consciously to disengage himself from his bodily desires and his human relationships. To do this, a Buddhist would be expected to give up high living — food, drink, sex — and spend much of his time studying and meditating. If he were successful, he would attain or at least draw near to Nirvana, or that wonderful state in which he would have ended his dependence on attachments or desires, a state of joyful and peaceful emptiness.

Indian, Chinese and Korean Buddhists, travelling over the seas but mostly through the Himalayas and into China from the west, crept from cave to cave, decorating many of them with beautiful paintings and statues, during the fifth through eighth centuries. It is curious why Buddhism would have appealed to the literal and sensible Chinese, who already had Confucius, and in its purest form, it wouldn't have. By the time Buddhism reached China, however, it was 1200 years old as a religion, and had changed considerably. It was more intellectual, more tolerant of other philosophies, and very rich, having an impressive literature and art and a lively group of Boddhisattvas, or half-gods, who lived as men or women and tried to help others. These Boddhisattvas gave Buddhism a colorful mythology, and also a compassionate air, which had lately been absent from the dry and rational Confucians. The highly ascetic life style was no longer insisted upon. In fact, the art and literature were quite sensual in nature.

Once in China, Buddhism found adherents even among the T'ang Empress Wu, an ex-concubine who was not content merely to rule behind the scenes, and who offered Buddhism a place in Chinese society. The splitting of the Buddhists into sects, in rivalry with each other, also led to growth in numbers. The Buddhist monasteries, places of refuge but also increasingly of wealth and beauty, finally caused the Chinese government to try to control the movement, and eventually it was officially persecuted. It never enjoyed official acceptance after the T'ang Dynasty, but it remained in China, in the form of temples, statues and a few adherents, until Communist times. Mao Tse-tung's mother, for example, was an ardent Buddhist.

Other visitors to China were Italians, the Polos, including the young Marco, who accompanied his father and uncle on a trading trip to China during the thirteenth century. There they gained the favor of the Khubilai Khan, the Mongol leader of China at that time, who allowed them to trade, and who sent Marco, who had learned Chinese and become very conversant with Chinese customs, out on governmental missions, especially to the south. The "barbaric" Mongols had offended the southerners with their horses, their pillage and their lack of sanitation, so Khubilai used the popular and observant westerner as a go-between. Polo and his family returned to Italy after seventeen years in China, when the approaching death of Khubilai made them fear that they would lose Mongol protection. Marco's memoirs were well-known in Europe, and inspired much of its later interest in China.

The Italian Jesuit, Matteo Ricci, and his retinue arrived later, in 1600. He is chiefly remembered as a Christian pioneer, yet there are suspicions that the Chinese may have been more interested in his astronomical equipment, maps, prisms, as well as his charm, dogmatic flexibility and knowledge of Chinese, than in what he told them of Christianity. His successor-Jesuits enjoyed great favor in the Chinese court for more than one hundred years, yet Catholicism never gained much of a foothold in China.

One reason why foreign ideas were not very interesting to the Chinese was that they considered themselves, and were considered by other Asians, to be the "mother lode" of Asian culture. Chinese language, Confucian ideology, and the artistic creations of the Chinese court were frankly copied in Korea, Japan and Vietnam, and influential among the Manchus and Mongols. "A love and veneration for Chinese characters has been a binding link between the various countries (in Asia)."* Since the characters are nonphonetic, they have been easily transferable to countries whose languages sound very different from Chinese.

China's relationship with all of these other countries was also maternal. Usually travellers from other countries, such as the famous Japanese diarist, Ennin, in the ninth century, felt awed by China. It was partly the feeling that Jews and Christians have when returning to Jerusalem, partly the appreciation of a large, durable, peaceful and meticulously ordered civilization.

As time went on, foreign travellers came in groups to China to offer gifts, which they called "tribute," to the Chinese Emperor, whom they, like the Chinese, considered to be the Son of Heaven. These were the long-standing tribute relations, which governed Chinese diplomacy for hundreds of years. The list of those countries acknowledging Chinese superiority and sending tribute to China grew long and impressive: during the Ming dynasty it included Korea, the Liu-ch'iu (Ryukyu) islands, Annam (North Vietnam), Champa (South Vietnam), Japan, Cambodia, Siam, Borneo, Java, Sumatra, certain states on the southeast coast of India, and even something called "Syria."** These elaborate missions of tribute acknowledged the vassalage of the "lesser states" toward China, as symbolized not only by the gifts, but also by an extended walk-and-kneel sequence called the "kotow" (literally, the three kneelings and the nine prostrations). They were not permanent embassies, but they did lead to the exchange of envoys, and to a considerable connection between China and her neighbors.

Why would other Asian countries want to establish their inferiority vis-a-vis China? Because China's long and centralized history, rich culture, and impressive language had really convinced them that she was what she claimed to be, the "center country." On a more practical level, they were eager for trade and the kind of military and diplomatic help that

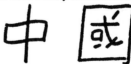

*Fairbank and Reischauer, East Asia: *The Great Tradition,* (Boston, 1960), p. 44.

**The nation is registered as Syria in Chinese records, but no more than that is known about it.

could occasionally come from China, or from the prestige of having relations with China. The attraction of the Chinese tea, porcelains, textiles and even weapons which were given as imperial "gifts in reply" to the original "tribute" was so great that at times traders from far away simply invented kingdoms from which to bring tribute! The Chinese themselves, benefiting from the trade, also felt that tribute relations regularized the frontier, kept them informed about developments in other countries, and extended their own version of culture and stabilization over a wider base.

All this was very well until the European traders came along in numbers. Having no sense of indebtedness to the Chinese language or philosophy, in fact considering them both to be downright peculiar, the Europeans were offended by the Chinese assumption of superiority, mystified by their desire for seclusion, and positively livid at the thought of the kotow.

The first major group of European traders to arrive were the Portuguese, who dominated the sixteenth century. They set up a base of sorts, in Macao, near Canton, but they were never sure of its legal status. The Dutch and English joined them in the Canton area in the seventeenth century. These men, eager for trade with the Chinese empire, fiercely competitive with each other and ill-supervised by their respective nations, were impatient with the slow and lofty attitude of the Chinese officials, who were following a clear "don't touch" policy, and who would let them trade only through specific merchant firms, called "hongs," in Canton. No trade was allowed in any other Chinese city. Not the most refined of characters even in their own countries, often dirty and women-starved after months at sea, the traders could not be said to represent European civilization at its best.

The Chinese considered them to be hairy, mutton-smelling, big-nosed, repulsive, even dangerous. Women shielded their babies lest a foreigner's glance make them sick. Western traders were isolated in special compounds from any Chinese except carefully screened servants. No foreigner, for example, was ever allowed inside the walled city of Canton.

For the British, the seriousness of their differences with the Chinese was only recognized in the latter part of the eighteenth century. By that time the British were eager to import Chinese tea, which was lighter and less bitter than the Indian variety. The East India Company, which had a monopoly on Chinese trade, was allowing itself to be pushed around by Cantonese officials, and was being challenged by several young and aggressive traders. It was felt that the British should expand their trade with China, and so the Earl of Macartney was appointed by the King of England to go to Peking, there to represent England in grand style, and preside over a new round of negotiations.

Lord Macartney studied and prepared well for his trip, and took along ninety-five people, including two Chinese Christians whom he found in Italy to act as interpreters. He brought along 600 gifts of various sizes to present to the Emperor. His specific requests of the Emperor were to expand the number of ports where westerners could trade with Chinese, to include some northern ones nearer to Peking, and to work out a systematic tariff approved by the Emperor himself, thus eliminating the extra gifts which Chinese officials expected. He also wanted to have an English minister in Peking, and generally to work out treaty relationships between two equal nations.

Arriving in Peking in 1793, he found the Ch'ien-lung Emperor to be eighty-three years old, but full of health, vigor and self-confidence. Chinese officials persistently referred to the gifts which Macartney had brought as tribute. Although he and the members of his party were treated with great respect, Macartney complained that they were kept off to themselves too much, and restricted in their movements; they were literally "prisoners in silken bonds." Macartney himself was expected to perform the kotow, but this he refused, explaining carefully that he could not possibly prostrate himself more for a foreign Emperor than he would be expected to do for his own sovereign. He agreed to kneel, but only on one knee. This mark of respect was accepted, and he was the first foreigner ever to be allowed into the Emperor's presence on that basis.*

On the question of the expansion of trade, however, Macartney found the Ch'ien-lung Emperor to be very firm. As he had written to George III a few years earlier (see the document at the end of this chapter), he could not understand why the British wanted to force arrangements on China which would be so contrary to her own customs. The two proud nations faced each other, in all their respective majesty — but then the British were scolded for impertinent behavior, and withdrew, somewhat abashed by the encounter.

In spite of frustrations about the trading arrangements, the British were soon joined by Americans, French and Russians in pursuit of the China trade, and the trade was brisk and lucrative. Chinese silk, porcelains and especially the newly popular tea found

*The Dutch had been willing to perform the kotow for years, and kept on doing it.

a ready market at home. The problem was exchange: what did the Chinese need and want which could be traded for what the westerners knew they needed and wanted? Earlier, the Chinese had imported cotton from India, but not in very large amounts. In the early nineteenth century matters came to a head on this issue. The drain of silver to China was becoming alarming, and the British East India Company lost its monopoly on trade in Canton, thus opening the field to comparatively uncontrolled private traders. An article of trade simply had to be found which would be considered valuable enough by the Chinese to restore the balance of trade. That article turned out to be opium.

Opium, fruit of the poppy, had been used for centuries, but was smoked only since smoking tobacco had been taught the white man by the Indians in Jamestown, Virginia. This led to its widespread use as a social habit. It is highly addictive, physically as well as psychologically, and quickly leads to a life in which it is the dominant experience. The Chinese smoked it most often through a water pipe. Having smoked, they felt very relaxed, enjoying colorful and exciting dreams, dreams in which they were very powerful or intelligent. Often they would compose whole poems or solve problems during their dreams, even remembering to write them down. The next morning, however, they wouldn't be able to read their own handwriting.

Scene in an Opium Den

Chinese demand for opium changed the balance of trade sharply. Soon Chinese silver was making up the difference between what the Chinese wanted and what the westerners wanted. From the westerners' point of view, opium is an excellent material for intercontinental trade. It has high value per unit of bulk, it travels well, requires little work on the ship captain's part, and yields high profit if kept in restricted supply. Official Chinese policy, of course, was dead against the trade, but the use of opium in China was spreading rapidly, among the officials and army as well as among the poor, and there were at least as many private traders on the Chinese side as on the European who were interested in the trade. British and Indian traders brought opium from India, largely from lands controlled by the British East India Company, while the Americans brought theirs from Turkey.

Besides these differences on the expansion of trade, equality between traders, and the open connivance in a forbidden trade, there was the issue of extraterritoriality. Western ideas about the rights of the individual were very different from the Chinese theory of mutual responsibility outlined in the last chapter. In several incidents which occurred during the early nineteenth century, such as the one in document #2 at the end of this chapter, the Chinese demanded that western sailors be turned over to the Chinese authorities for justice, Chinese style. They were considered "responsible" even for accidental killings, and duly punished, usually by strangling, in a straight "life for life" equation. Proof wasn't what the westerners insisted it should be; methods used, including torture, also offended them. Finally, there was always the well-founded suspicion that the "barbarian" would be discriminated against in a Chinese court of law.

Usual international procedure is that a foreigner in any country must behave as the nationals must behave, or face the same consequences: "when in Rome do as the Romans do." But westerners in China came to believe that China's expectations were too bizarre, her hostility too ready, her methods of justice too Byzantine, for a foreigner ever to manage successfully to live under Chinese law. Finally they demanded that western nationals be allowed to live under the jurisdiction of their own country's laws, even when they were in China. By the early nineteenth century, the British flatly refused to hand over their nationals to Chinese justice. Although the Chinese didn't believe that the British had this right, they let them get away with it.

As in the period under Lord Macartney, the British nearly fifty years later were also interested in putting an end to the old tribute relations and in substituting them with new relationships based on equality between governmental representatives, freedom to travel, to meet the rulers, to talk and persuade and explore within another's country. The British, like many other nineteenth century westerners, felt superior to the Chinese and to others from Asia or Africa. But in the 1830's they were much more interested in trade than in war.

The Chinese government, too, seemed to have been avoiding war. Although it must have been clear to them for decades that the illicit opium trade in China was growing to alarming proportions, they seemed not to see it. Concerned southern Chinese were even worried that the government saw opium as a way to pacify and control the hot-tempered southerners, who had always been the most resistant to Manchu authority. But in 1839, the Chinese court, deciding to crack down on the opium trade and convinced that the sticky-handed officials in Canton weren't up to the assignment, sent an incorruptible and strong official, Commissioner Lin Tse-hsu, to get the job done. Lin came to the post with an excellent background. A brilliant scholar, able to compose complicated poetry at a moment's notice, he had served in various parts of China, and had had experience with the British, with smugglers — of salt — and with people who were trying to rid themselves of the opium habit. His diary as he proceeded southward to Canton from Peking is filled with reverence for the Emperor, interest in his surroundings, and an abhorrence for either luxury or for any extra gifts which might be given to himself or to his servants.

Within a week after Lin's arrival one could sense a change in the atmosphere. He was asked to focus exclusively on the opium trade, and was determined to gain control over both the Chinese and the western sides of the trade at once. He addressed the Chinese by tightening up on "corruption" in its many forms, such as the long-standing habit of the Chinese marines, when they infrequently captured some of the outlawed opium, to keep a part of it for their own use. Lin also wrote letters to the Cantonese people, insulting them for their indulgence of the trade, but also promising them that it was a habit that could be given up. "Last year, when I was Governor-General of Hupeh and Hunan, there was a man who had been an addict for thirty years and smoked an ounce a day. But he managed to give it up, and immediately his cheeks began to fill out and the strength came back to his limbs. I saw the same thing happen in case after case. How can anyone suppose that a habit which can be given up in other provinces cannot be given up in Kwangtung?"* Lin also instructed all teachers to organize their students into pao chia groups, the better to watch each other for the sale or use of opium. He worked with the gentry to set up "collection centers" where Chinese could turn in their opium and pipes.

For the foreigners, Lin devised a similar mixture of the command and virtue ethics, of the use of force and persuasion. He wrote a letter to Queen Victoria, included in the documents at the end of this chapter, which urged her to think of what the trade was doing to the Chinese people and to control her side as effectively as the Chinese Emperor was prepared to do. He tried to determine which were the most dangerous of the foreign traders, and to treat them especially harshly while he tried to stay on somewhat friendly terms with the others. Finally, when nothing else seemed to work, he ordered all the foreign merchants who were in Canton to surrender all of their opium. Besides that, he wanted a promise that they would not sell any more. He surrounded the foreign warehouses with Chinese troops, put chains across the river which they had to travel to reach Canton, and threatened that all trade of any kind would stop unless his demands were met. When the British complied with his order, finally giving up 20,000 chests, Lin saw that all the opium was limed and dumped ceremoniously into the harbor!

The destruction of their property was bad enough; what also upset the British was Lin's insistence on the promise to give up the trade in the future. They felt that he was asking them to tie the hands of future commercial policy makers. The restriction of certain of their nationals and the intimidation of them and their servants also caused much local tension between the foreigners and Commissioner Lin. Opium being a somewhat embarrassing topic over which to fight, they widened the issues as much as possible. Finally in July 1839 there was another extraterritoriality flare-up, when some drunken British and American sailors killed a Chinese peasant near the port at Kowloon, and the Chinese authorities demanded that one of them be isolated from the others by the British and given up to Chinese justice. The British flatly refused to give a culprit up to Lin and the newly emboldened Americans, who had never before dared to defy the Chinese authorities in this respect, also went along with them. But the Chinese now cut off all food supplies, and the British had to leave the Canton area; they found an excellent place to camp in the deserted island of Hong

*Arthur Waley, *The Opium War Through Chinese Eyes,* (Stanford, California, 1958), p. 24.

Kong, just outside the Canton harbor. It was a barren, rocky place, but it had an excellent harbor, and the Chinese officials were out of sight. Tentative negotiations were opened. Meanwhile, the opium trade continued briskly.

What the Chinese didn't know, and the British knew, or at least hoped, was that help would soon arrive from the British navy. There were small skirmishes between the traders and the Chinese during the winter of 1839-1840, but the decisive battles were the next summer, when a British expeditionary force arrived. The conflict was now officially between nations. The foreigners quickly displayed their superior western firepower. The Chinese were amazed at the western ships' maneuverability; as Lin put it in a private letter to a friend:

> "The rebels' ships on the open sea came and went as they pleased, now in the south and now suddenly in the north, changing successively between morning and evening. If we tried to put up a defense everywhere, not only would we toil and expend ourselves without limit, but also how could we recruit and transport so many troops, militia, artillery, and ammunition, and come to their support quickly?"*

As might be expected of a nation which purported to use reason rather than force as a way of persuading people to do what was right, the Chinese army was small, badly organized, and had become demoralized since the days of K'ang-Hsi Emperor. Their equipment was antiquated, and they had little help from local people, who were apathetic. Furthermore, as a foreign dynasty, the Manchus were themselves in an insecure position and could not ask the Chinese to suffer too long or too much.

Commissioner Lin Tse-hsu, who only months earlier had been offered the prestigious Kiangsi Governor-Generalship as soon as he had finished dealing with the opium threat in Canton, was now in disgrace. The imperial edict read: "Because Lin Tse-hsu, having been sent to Canton to manage military and foreign affairs, failed to bring either task to a successful conclusion, both he and the former Governor-General Teng, having merited the severest penalty, are to proceed to I-li (on the northwest frontier) and there do what they can to expiate their crimes."**

By 1842 the Chinese were ready to negotiate for peace, though "negotiate" seems too strong a word to describe a process by which the Chinese were simply forced to grant the British nearly

*Teng and Fairbank, *China's Response to the West,* (New York, 1963), p. 28.
**Waley, p. 155.

everything they asked for. The treaties between the westerners and the Chinese during the nineteenth century were always referred to as "unequal treaties" by the Chinese, who always seemed to give much more than they got. As part of the first of these "unequal treaties," the Treaty of Nanking, the British were allowed by the Chinese to expand the number of the so-called "treaty ports" (ports in which they would be allowed to carry on trade), from one to five: Amoy, Foochow, Ningpo and Shanghai were added to the list. The Chinese agreed to pay an indemnity of 21 million Mexican dollars to pay for the destroyed opium as well as expenses to the British and the payment of debts owed the British traders. Hong Kong, the island used as a base of operations all through the war, was now ceded to the British. The old "hong" monopolies were abolished, so that the westerners could now trade with any Chinese firm which offered good wares and good prices. Furthermore, the Chinese promised that their tariff would be fair and uniform, and not raised unless both sides agreed to the change.

Essentially, this agreement took away China's ability to set its own tariffs, and was thus a tremendous infringement on China's sovereignty. Another infringement was the Chinese agreement that the British would have extraterritorial jurisdiction over their own subjects while they were in China. These two provisions, more than any of the others, were considered tremendously insulting by patriotic Chinese at the time, and especially so in later decades.

The British were not the only western nation to win new privileges in China. One of the clauses in the treaty stated that:

> ". . . should the Emperor, hereafter, from any cause whatever, be pleased to grant additional privileges or immunities to any of the subjects or Citizens of such Foreign Countries, the same privileges and immunities will be extended to and enjoyed by British Subjects."

Other nations scurried to adopt this "most-favored-nation clause," with the result that any concession to one of them was gained by all. This clause undermined the Chinese attempt to "divide the barbarians."

Finally, the British put an end to the old tribute relations language. They insisted that from then on, any message addressed to the Chinese Emperor would be referred to as a communication, not a petition. In language, the two nations, England and China, could now be considered equals. In strength, it had now been revealed that Britain was by far the stronger, that it was prepared to use its strength against China, and that there were several other nations which would work with Britain if necessary to force China to back down.

One would think that the years just after the Treaty of Nanking would have been blissful for the British traders, almost like Macartney's dream. But they were not. First of all, the status of opium had never really been agreed upon. Second, the Chinese were still adopting a "don't touch" attitude about foreign contact, travel in China, or access to Peking. Those in the treaty ports clung to the edge of the continent, dreaming of the riches which might be within, of the profits, as they put it, in "the adding of an inch to the Chinaman's coat-tail." Finally, although the Chinese had agreed to certain concessions in theory, in practice their policy seemed to be one of delay and diversion. The memorandum on "Methods for Handling the Barbarians" which is reproduced at the end of this chapter reveals these tactics, as well as an attitude of disgust and intolerance felt toward westerners.

Thus in spite of all of the trouble they had taken to clear up outstanding grievances with the Chinese, the British began to wonder if they had really won the war after all.

An Example of Chinese Diplomacy: Ch'ien-Lung's Letter to George III

You, O King, from afar have yearned after the blessings of our civilization, and in your eagerness to come into touch with our converting influence, have sent an Embassy across the sea bearing a memorial . . .

Hitherto, all European nations, including your own country's barbarian merchants, have carried on their trade with our Celestial Empire at Canton. Such has been the procedure for many years, although our Celestial Empire possesses all things in prolific abundance and lacks no product within its own borders. There was therefore no need to import the manufactures of outside barbarians in exchange for our own produce. But as the tea, silk and porcelain which the Celestial Empire produces, are absolute necessities to European nations and to yourselves, we have permitted, as a signal mark of favour, that foreign hongs should be established at Canton, so that your wants might be supplied and your country thus participate in our beneficence. But your Ambassador (Lord Macartney) has now put forward new requests which completely fail to recognize the Throne's principle to "treat strangers from afar with indulgence," and to exercise a pacifying control over barbarian tribes the world over. Moreover, our dynasty, swaying the myriad races of the globe, extends the same benevolence towards all. Your England is not the only nation trading at Canton. If other nations, following your bad example, wrongfully importune my ear with further impossible requests, how will it be possible for me to treat them with easy indulgence? Nevertheless, I do not forget the lonely remoteness of your island, cut off from the world by intervening wastes of sea, nor do I overlook your excusable ignorance of the usages of our Celestial Empire . . .

I have even gone out of my way to grant any requests which were in any way consistent with Chinese usage. Above all, upon you, who . . . have shown your submissive loyalty by sending this tribute mission, I have heaped benefits far in excess of those accorded to other nations. But the demands presented by your Embassy are not only a contravention of dynastic tradition, but would be utterly unproductive of good result to yourself, besides being quite impracticable . . . If, after the receipt of this explicit decree, you lightly give ear to the representations of your subordinates and allow your barbarian merchants to proceed to Chekiang and Tientsin, with the object of landing and trading there, the ordinances of my Celestial Empire are strict in the extreme, and the local officials, both civil and military, are bound reverently to obey the law of the land. Should your vessels touch the shore, your merchants will assuredly never be permitted to land or reside there, but will be subject to instant expulsion . . . Do not say that you were not warned in time! Tremblingly obey and show no negligence! A special mandate!

Hellerman and Stein, *China: Readings on the Middle Kingdom,* (Simon and Schuster, Inc., New York, 1971), pp. 145-147.

Terranova: An Extraterritorial Tale

There was once an Italian sailor called Terranova, who worked on an American ship, the Emily, chartered in Baltimore but also working out of Salem, Massachusetts. Terranova was swabbing the decks one day in Canton harbor, when a Chinese woman, standing on her little junk which was perched up against the ship, began to call to him. He was angry at the way the Chinese edged up against the ship; they had been asked not to, several times. He also obviously didn't understand what she was saying, and after a while her persistent calling to him began to get on his nerves. At some point, either by accident or perhaps otherwise, Terranova's jug, which was standing on the rail full of water to use in his swabbing, fell off the rail and landed on or near the woman below. She fell into the water, and, because she was stunned and also didn't know how to swim, she drowned.

A life had been lost; Chinese authorities believed that harmony would not return until something had been done to redress the balance. They therefore demanded that Terranova should be given up to the Chinese authorities for determination of what his responsibility had been for her death, and also possible punishment. The captain of the Emily, believing in Terranova's violent protestations that the whole thing had been an accident, doubted the ability of the Chinese to give Terranova a fair trial as he understood it. He also felt that he ought, as captain, to act as if he were a father to Terranova. If you were the captain of the Emily, what would you do? And for what reasons?

Lin Tse-hsu's Letter to Queen Victoria

A communication: magnificently our great Emperor soothes and pacifies China and the foreign countries, regarding them all with the same kindness. If there is profit, then he shares it with the peoples of the world. This is because he takes the mind of heaven and earth as his mind.

The kings of your honorable country by a tradition handed down from generation to generation have always been noted for their politeness and submissiveness. We have read your successive tributary memorials saying, "In general our countrymen who go to trade in China have always received His Majesty the Emperor's gracious treatment and equal justice," and so on. Privately we are delighted with the way in which the honorable rulers of your country deeply understand the grand principles and are grateful for the Celestial grace. For this reason the Celestial Court in soothing those from afar has redoubled its polite and kind treatment. The profit from trade has been enjoyed by them continuously for two hundred years. This is the source from which your country has become known for its wealth.

But after a long period of commercial intercourse, there appear among the crowd of barbarians both good persons and bad, unevenly. Consequently there are those who smuggle opium to seduce the Chinese people and so cause the spread of the poison to all provinces. Such persons who only care to profit themselves, and disregard their harm to others, are not tolerated by the laws of heaven and are unanimously hated by human beings. His Majesty the Emperor, upon hearing of this, is in a towering rage. He has especially sent me, his commissioner, to come to Kwangtung, and together with the governor-general and governor jointly to investigate and settle this matter.

Having established the new regulations, we presume that the ruler of your honorable country, who takes delight in our culture and whose disposition is inclined toward us, must be able to instruct the various barbarians to observe the law with care. It is only necessary to explain to them the advantages and disadvantages and then they will know that the legal code of the Celestial Court must be absolutely obeyed with awe.

We find that your country is sixty or seventy thousand li from China. Yet there are barbarian ships that strive to come here for trade for the purpose of making a great profit. The wealth of

China is used to profit the barbarians. That is to say, the great profit made by the barbarians is all taken from the rightful share of China. By what right do they then in return use the poisonous drug to injure the Chinese people? Even though the barbarians may not necessarily intend to do us harm, yet in coveting profit to an extreme they have no regard for injuring others. Let us ask, where is your conscience? I have heard that the smoking of opium is very strongly forbidden by your country; that is because the harm caused by opium is clearly understood. Since it is not permitted to do harm to your own country, then even less should you let it be passed on to the harm of other countries – how much less to China! Of all that China exports to foreign countries, there is not a single thing which is not beneficial to people: they are of benefit when eaten, or of benefit when used, or of benefit when resold: all are beneficial. Is there a single article from China which has done any harm to foreign countries? Take tea and rhubarb, for example: the foreign countries cannot get along for a single day without them. If China cuts off these benefits without sympathy for those who are going to suffer, then what can the barbarians rely upon to keep themselves alive? Moreover the woolens, camlets, and longells (i.e. textiles) of foreign countries cannot be woven unless they obtain Chinese silk. If China, again, cuts off this beneficial export, what profit can the barbarians expect to make? As for other foodstuffs, beginning with candy, ginger, cinnamon, and so forth, and articles for use, beginning with silk, satin, chinaware, and so on, all the things that must be had by foreign countries are innumerable. On the other hand, articles coming from the outside to China can be used only as toys. We can take them or get along without them. Since they are not needed by China, what difficulty would there be if we closed the frontier and stopped the trade? Nevertheless, our Celestial Court lets tea, silk, and other goods be shipped without limit and circulated everywhere without begrudging it in the slightest. This is for no other reason but to share the benefit with the people of the whole world.

The Cantonese Denunciate the British

The thoroughly loyal and patriotic people of the whole province of Kwantung instruct the rebellious barbarian dogs and sheep for their information. We note that you English barbarians have formed the habits and developed the nature of wolves, plundering and seizing things by force . . . In trade relations, you come to our country merely to covet profit. What knowledge do you have? Your seeking profit resembles the animal's greed for food. You are ignorant of our laws and institutions, ignorant of right principles . . . You have no gratitude for the great favor of our Celestial Court; on the contrary you treat us like enemies and do us harm. You use opium to injure our common people, cheating us of our silver and cash . . . Although you have penetrated our inland rivers and enticed fellows who renounce their fathers and their ruler to become Chinese traitors and stir up trouble among us, you are only using money to buy up their services – what good points have you? . . . Except for your ships being solid, your gunfire fierce, and your rockets powerful, what other abilities have you? . . .

Chinese Methods for Handling the Barbarians

From a memorial which was sent to the Emperor in 1844: (the author refers to himself in the third person)

He is mindful that the English barbarians were finally brought to the point of reconciliation in August 1842, and the American and French barbarians have also followed in their footsteps in the summer and autumn of the present year. Throughout this period of three years the barbarian situation has undergone deceptive changes in many respects and has not produced a unified development. The methods by which to conciliate the barbarians and get them under control similarly could not but shift about and change their form. Certainly we have to curb them by sincerity, but it has been even more necessary to control them by skillful methods. There are times when it is possible to have them follow our directions but not let them understand the reasons. Sometimes we expose everything so that they will not be suspicious, whereupon we can dissipate their rebellious restlessness. Sometimes we have given them receptions and entertainment, after which they have had a feeling of appreciation. And at still other times we have shown trust in them in a broad-minded way and deemed it unnecessary to go deeply into minute discussions with them, whereupon we have been able to get their help with the business at hand.

This is because the barbarians are born and grow up outside the frontiers of China, so that there are many things in the institutional system of the Celestial Dynasty with which they are not fully acquainted. Moreover, they are constantly making arbitrary interpretations of things, and it is difficult to enlighten them by means of reason.

(He goes on to describe the various customs of the barbarians, such as their banquets) . . . Moreover, the barbarians commonly lay great stress on their women. Whenever they have a distinguished guest, the wife is certain to come out to meet him . . . Your slave was confounded and ill at ease, . . . (but) the customs of the various Western countries cannot be regulated according to the ceremonies of the Middle Kingdom. If we should abruptly rebuke them, it would not be a way of shattering their stupidity and might give rise to their suspicion and dislike.

Furthermore, the various barbarians have come to live at peace and in harmony with us. We must give them some sort of entertainment and cordial reception; but we are on guard against an intimate relationship . . . with them. (We must never take any gifts from them) . . .

As to these various countries, although they have rulers, they may be either male or female, and they may rule variously for a long or a short time, all of which is far beyond the bounds of any system of laws. For example, the English barbarians are ruled by a female, the Americans and the French are ruled by males, the English and the French rulers both rule for life, while the ruler of the American barbarians is established by the campaigning of his countrymen, and is changed once in four years – after he leaves the position, he is of equal rank with the common people! . . . With this type of people from outside the bounds of civilization, who are blind and unawakened in styles of address and forms of ceremony, if we adhered to the proper forms in official documents and let them be weighed according to the status of superior and inferior, even though our tongues were dry and our throats parched (from urging them to follow our way), still they could not avoid closing their ears and acting as if deaf. Not only would there be no way to bring them to their senses, but also it would immediately cause friction. Truly it would be of no advantage in the essential business of subduing and conciliating them. To fight with them over empty names and get no substantial result would not be so good as to pass over these small matters and achieve our larger scheme . . .

(Vermilion endorsement: They could only be managed in this way. We thoroughly understand it.)

T'eng and Fairbank, *China's Response to the West,* (Harvard University Press, 1963), pp. 24-27 and 37-40.

4

Problems with the West

From 1842, when they first learned that they did not have the ability to stop the western encroachment on China by moral suasion and superior culture, the Manchus played a devious and desperate game right to the end of the dynasty in 1912. The only effective answer to western greed for markets and, later, raw imperial power, would have been a new dynasty or a newly strengthened Ch'ing dynasty, willing to undertake China's modernization on its own. The Manchus obviously didn't want the first, and they were only tentatively willing to explore the second. Instead, they preferred to expend their energies defensively instead of offensively, blaming the West instead of taking the initiative for modernizing China themselves.

In many ways this was an understandable reaction, and in some ways a wise one. To resist change was to endear oneself to the conservative scholar bureaucracy. Moreover, many of the troubles China was having clearly *did* come from the West. Although the willingness of so many Chinese to experiment with opium addiction has to be blamed primarily on their lack of opportunity and fulfillment in any life but fantasy, still the traders who supplied the opium could be blamed at least for its rapid spread over China. The trade was not legalized in spite of British petitions to that effect, and so during the 1840's and 1850's, while the trade doubled in size, and "receiving stations" grew up all over the Chinese coast, both the western and Chinese officials pretended not to notice its existence. In time, domestic production of opium replaced trade as its source, but the Chinese preferred foreign opium for its "kick." They believed that the strength and potential destructiveness in it could not have been produced in China's relatively benevolent soil!

The effect on China was alarming. Much of the culture was literally "high" for a century; officials were confused, merchants closed up shop early, armies dreamed through battles. A constant search for money to pay for those dreams led gentry families to sell off land, businesses to squander instead of reinvesting profits, and the corruption of government workers, especially the lowest level workers in the yamen, to grow astronomically during the nineteenth century. Of course decadence and hopelessness have the same symptoms as drug addiction and they can easily be mistaken for one another. But at any rate, these symptoms, for which the westerners were at least partly responsible, compounded other Chinese problems.

There was also the problem of overpopulation. Could this honestly be blamed on the westerners? Not in a literal sense, but it *is* true that the population spurt in China, from about 200 million in 1730 to 400 million in 1840, occurred partly because of improved strains of rice, partly through entirely new crops, such as potatoes, sweet potatoes, corn, peanuts and kaoliang, which were introduced by westerners through Canton. The peace and stability of a long-lived dynasty, and its improvement of transportation facilities, which helped the population survive local famines, was responsible for the rest of the rise in population.

You may say, "If there's enough to eat, why worry about a rising population?" This is true, but as the food supply rose, the population rose even faster. Also, populations don't live on bread alone. They need houses, roads, land, a local government which really knows what is happening, a sense of security as well as change, an orderly system of taxation and trade. Ancient governing methods, such as moral exhortations and the *pao chia,* couldn't handle these new pressures. Furthermore, the resources for governing, ever-shrinking because of poverty and the "squeeze," had to be stretched over a longer and longer list of responsibilities as well as a large population.

A rise in population is often accompanied by a rise in economic activity, which helps to alleviate the burden of the higher number, and actually is able to harness their energies in a way which leads to still more growth and a higher standard of living for all. But China for many centuries had been based on a static economy, one which has been called an "economy of scarcity."*

Since land was the one fixed value, and since the amount of arable land was relatively constant, the Chinese gave up the idea of progress early in their history and concentrated instead on survival. American parents raise their children to believe that "more is better;" but in China, children learned that "enough is plenty." One learned to be content with what one could produce for oneself; one didn't *need* metal implements, a varied diet, or even a

*By Fei Hsiao-tung, quoted by John K. Fairbank, *The United States and China,* (Cambridge, 1971), p. 236.

greater amount of productivity around the farm. Money was not even used most of the time, and was distrusted and feared by many. Reinvestment of any surplus that might exist was rare. It implied a future orientation, a belief in expansion or in technology, a feeling that man might produce more and have a higher standard of living then he had had before. It could lead to greed, restlessness, inattention to ritual or to family. All of this seemed like heresy to the Chinese peasant.

There were other weaknesses in the Chinese economy besides this attitude toward growth. Government monopoly over staples like salt and tea prevented the aggressive development of those fields. The Chinese didn't follow the custom of primogeniture, or leaving their entire estates to the eldest son; instead, they split up their holdings among all the sons in the next generation. This increased the insecurity of the family as an economic unit because of the constant breakup of landholdings into smaller and smaller units. Moreover, the existence of a "clan mentality" (whatever needs to be done, we can probably find someone in the clan to do it), meant that the best man was not always found for the job, or that needy relatives took precedence over money-making in any major decision.

The cleverest sons were made into scholars, and there was no second-son slot, such as existed in the West, for a career in business or the army. Both were looked down on as essentially unproductive, contrasted with farming. Although many women worked hard, footbinding cut out much of their productivity. Trade was considered parasitical. Confucius himself had mightily distrusted the word "profit."

At the edge of this relatively static economy were the bustling treaty ports, which during the 1840's and 1850's oversaw a tremendous growth in tea and silk, paid for mostly with money gained from the unacknowledged opium. British traders who were frustrated at how slowly the Chinese demand for British cotton grew tended to blame the likin, the Chinese taxes levied on goods in transit. Believers as they were in the noble qualities inherent in free trade, the British simply couldn't understand why the Chinese didn't crack down on these taxes, and they suspected corruption everywhere. The real reason why the Chinese peasant didn't buy more British cotton was that he was too poor even to consider it. But the western trader, already a self-appointed expert on China, watching money change hands and the number of firms in each treaty port climb sharply, and hearing tales about the opulence of the Imperial City in Peking, remained cut off from the real conditions in the interior.

In spite of the prosperity, there were problems even in the treaty ports. One had to do with the widespread piracy along the Chinese coast, which bothered the western traders a great deal, but about which the Ch'ing dynasty, which had enough to cope with, did nothing. Finally, in the late forties, the British themselves undertook to rid China of the pirates. All they succeeded in doing, however, was to force their relocation inland, farther up the Chinese rivers, especially the West River which runs through Canton.

Another problem had to do with the rush on the part of certain Chinese to join the westerners. Starting with servants and followed then by the Chinese firms which organized themselves in alliance with the treaty port trade, more and more Chinese sought to have themselves registered as linked to the foreigners, sometimes even gaining the status of extraterritoriality, which they often abused. Some wore western dress, and moved around the treaty ports with their western protectors and friends. They obviously constituted a threat not only to local government authorities, but also to local Chinese merchants, thus causing considerable division in the Chinese community.

The Coolie trade was also at its height during the 1840's and 1850's. Coolies was the word used to describe young male laborers who were shipped under contract to many parts of the world, but mostly to southeast Asia. The methods of recruitment, the promises made but not kept, and the conditions of the voyage, as well as the break up of the families and the loss of strong young workers, all combined to upset the Chinese. The Manchu government refused to admit that any emigration on any terms could be occurring. The British government tried to curb the worst abuses, but westerners were still blamed for the trade itself, as they invariably supplied the transport.

Finally, there was the problem of the missionaries, who between 1842 and 1860 were confined to the treaty ports, but who used their base there to make contacts in the interior and to spread their movement. The Chinese blamed the West for the confusion and pain caused by the abundance of western ideas which entered China during the nineteenth century. New ideas can be very dangerous; entertain just one, and your previously connected assumptions might topple over like a line of dominoes. Western ideas — on Christ, on the essential importance and equality of each individual, on the potential benefits of science and technology — were especially dangerous at a time in which a beleaguered dynasty's only source of support was a conservative bureaucracy.

Christianity was the most threatening of all the new ideas at that point. The whole idea of a literal "Son of God," not to mention his physical resurrection, sounded irrational. Christ's ideas on ethics — the Sermon on the Mount, for example — resembled Confucian humanism, but the form of Christianity which was exported in the missionary movement during the nineteenth century tended to be dogmatic and theological, rather than casual and ethical.

Medical missionaries such as Peter Parker combined service to the heathen (including Commissioner Lin Tse-hsu, who in 1839 was fitted with a truss for his hernia)* with preaching which was designed to save his soul, hopefully in time. During the middle of the century, although mostly confined to treaty ports, some Catholic missions had been founded inland, where they took care of orphans, opened schools, and developed a Chinese Christian following, disparaged by some as "rice Christians." Although more geographically extensive, the Catholics were more willing to compromise than were the Protestants. They were long-gowned and scholarly, like the Confucians. The Protestants, who remained vigilantly their own men, ended by making a bigger impression on the Chinese. It was all as well-meaning as it was overbearing, yet one can understand why the Chinese resented it.

By the early 1850's the disgusted British were eager to clear up the disagreements which had led to such confrontations between the westerners and the Chinese. The westerners, however, had very little faith in the newest Manchu Emperor. As one of them put it:

> Should an Emperor arise among them possessed of a great intellect, a will of iron, a reformer determined to initiate his people into the progressive civilization of the West, we believe that the work of regeneration would proceed with rapid strides . . .
>
> (But) the Young Mantchou (sic) prince who in 1850 ascended the Imperial throne, will probably not be the great and powerful reformer of whom we have spoken. He commenced his reign by degrading and putting to death the statesmen who, during that of his predecessor, had seen themselves compelled, under the English cannon, to make some concessions to the Europeans.
>
> . . . Every device has been tried to elude the obligation of treaties . . .

*Edward V. Gulick, *Peter Parker and the Opening of China,* (Cambridge, 1973), p. 89.

It is evident to the least clear-sighted, that the object of the Manchou government is to disgust Europeans, and break off all intercourse with them; it would gladly have nothing to do with them at any price.*

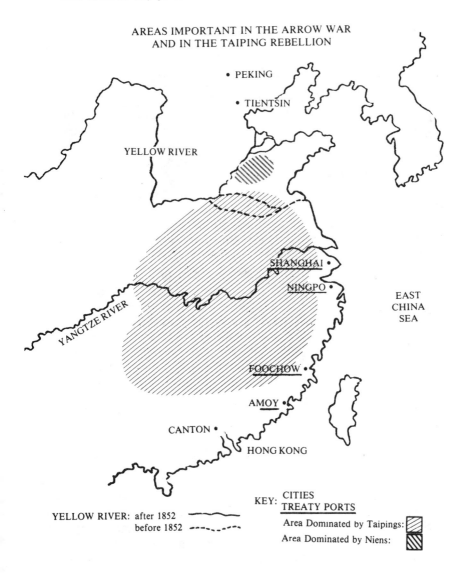

AREAS IMPORTANT IN THE ARROW WAR
AND IN THE TAIPING REBELLION

• PEKING

• TIENTSIN

YELLOW RIVER

SHANGHAI •

NINGPO •

EAST
CHINA
SEA

YANGTZE RIVER

FOOCHOW •

AMOY •

CANTON •

HONG KONG

KEY: CITIES
TREATY PORTS

YELLOW RIVER: after 1852 ⎯⎯⎯
before 1852 ⎯·⎯·⎯·⎯

Area Dominated by Taipings:
Area Dominated by Niens:

*M. Huc, *A Journey Through The Chinese Empire*, 2 vols., (New York, 1895), 1:412-13.

The young Hsien-feng Emperor of whom the observer spoke was weak, anti-foreign, and too absorbed in his food, drink and large number of concubines to have much energy left over for China. In this atmosphere arose two events of great magnitude and threat to the Manchu throne: the Arrow War and the Taiping Rebellion.

The Arrow War was the natural result of all of the profits as well as the misunderstandings of the 1840's and 1850's: the British and French were doing well in China, but they wanted to do even better. They had been pressuring the Chinese authorities for a revision of the Treaty of Nanking for years, but these officials always claimed that they weren't the ones to negotiate new treaties, or they refused to meet for even preliminary talks, claiming to be too busy. The westerners grew more and more frustrated with the Chinese style, as well as with their specific grievances. Also contributing to a general European feeling that the time was ripe for another war were their fears about the Hsien-feng Emperor and their realization that the Taiping Rebellion, which had already begun, would weaken the dynasty and render it more apt to give in to their demands.

This was the general atmosphere, and it probably contributed more than anything to the war; but the "causes" of the war are usually cited differently. In 1856 the British found an incident worth fighting for when a Chinese owned naval vessel, registered in Hong Kong and therefore holding extraterritorial rights, was detained and "defiled" (in other words, its British flag was taken down) by the Chinese government. The French, too, were incensed at the time because one of their missionaries, Father Chapdelaine, had been found outside a treaty port, accused of being a rebel, tortured and killed. Over these issues the English and French, in a rare act of cooperation, went to war against the Chinese. After several delays, they took over Canton and began ruling it, but they were not able to get big concessions out of the throne until they threatened Tientsin in 1858. Even then, once the westerners went away again, the Chinese refused to ratify or honor the Treaties of Tientsin to which they had earlier agreed. The British and French then returned in 1860 with an even larger force, and marched to Peking, forcing the Emperor to flee to Manchuria. The situation was chaotic. Both sides had their more radical and more moderate elements, and had to spend as much energy controlling each other as facing the enemy. Certain Britishers were captured, even as they were negotiating in good faith; in revenge, the Emperor's summer palace was burned and vandalized. Finally, in 1860, in the Peking

Convention, a settlement was once again reached, but this time the Chinese had to pay even more dearly for their peace. The result was more indemnity, more concession of land to the British (Kowloon peninsula, on the Chinese mainland across from Hong Kong), and more treaty ports opened. Foreigners were given the right to trade on the Yangtze river itself, rights to travel were increased, missionaries were to be allowed to travel outside the treaty ports, where they would be protected by the Chinese authorities, opium was legalized, and the western nations would henceforth be allowed to maintain legations at Peking. Furthermore, because of the "most-favored nation" clauses, the Americans and Russians obtained as many concessions as the British and French.

The second round of treaties at this time was a logical continuation of the Treaty of Nanking. Again, the westerners were proving that the command ethic was at least one way to force a revolution on China. But China during the years between the late forties and the early sixties was engaged in another kind of revolution as well, the Taiping Rebellion.

The Taiping Rebellion was started in the 1840's when a young Hakka scholar named Hung Hsiu-ch'uan came to believe, after a very graphic dream, that God had called him and that he was actually the younger brother of Jesus. When he first began preaching, his contact with Christianity was actually very limited as he had only talked briefly with one missionary and had read one pamphlet in Chinese. His own philosophy and behavior, moreover, were much more colored by the harsh tone of some of the Old Testament stories than by the gentle spirituality of the New Testament. But Hung based his position on his relationship with the God of Jesus, and to the Chinese this made him (and his rebellion) definitely a Christian and western phenomenon.

As a Hakka, Hung already felt apart from the rest of the Chinese. As one of China's earliest important nationalists, he resented the Manchus' leadership of China. As a three-time examination failer, he was at loose ends, and harbored a sense both of disappointment in himself and of anger at "the system." His teachings and sense of mission had already proclaimed him as special and he proposed radical reforms, yet there was at first little action behind his words. His followers were scattered along the West River near Canton, but were not connected or militant.

The real meaning behind the rebellion, therefore, came when it was translated from sermons to a secret society, and finally into coherent military plans, a process reflecting, more than anything else, the pervasive insecurity of the times. Bandits were so common in South China in the 1840's that the Taipings were forced to hire guards for their temples, and to fight in other feuds from which they could expect no justice from the authorities. To be fair, one must admit that the Taipings were often a rowdy bunch who had also engaged in destruction of the idols in *others'* temples, which was one reason why they were involved in so many feuds! At any rate, as the military aspect of the religion grew, so did the movement as a whole. In 1851 Hung chose a dynastic title, *T'ai-p'ing T'ien-kuo,* or the Heavenly Kingdom of Great Peace, and marched north to claim the Mandate. As the Taipings marched, they were joined by bored soldiers, homeless peasants, out-of-work pirates, and secret society members upset by the new trade routes. They made an impressive showing against the disorganized Manchu armies, who were both under-supplied and mostly unwilling to fight. When the Taipings reached the Yangtze River, they set sail towards the sea in a vast flotilla, finally stopping at Nanking (translated the "southern capital"), where they set up their government.

In 1853 the course of the Yellow River was dramatically altered during a massive flood. The mouth of the river was moved northward by 200 miles (see map on page 53). This seemed to many to be a heavenly sign that the end of the dynasty was approaching. The Taipings sent forces from Nanking, entered sixteen out of China's eighteen provinces, and captured 600 walled cities. As John Fairbank points out, the dynasty's ". . . 'victories', which every imperial commander was bound by custom to report to the throne, occurred closer and closer to Peking."* The Taipings were a thorn in the side of the Manchus all through the 1850's and early 1860's.

The Taiping Rebellion illustrated both the desperation of life in an overpopulated, impoverished and poorly led society, and the dynamite which new ideas, however poorly understood, can introduce into such a situation. Today the Communists, who share much with the Taipings, claim that the rebellion illustrated something else as well: the "true socialistic spirit" which had long resided in the Chinese masses.

Further research is needed before the Communists' claim can be validated or disproved, as it is difficult to tell what the attraction of the Taipings' plans was for the ordinary people. But their plans deserve further study, for many were radical departures from the society which existed in traditional China.

Some of the Taipings' hopes were to end footbinding and child

*Fairbank, *The United States and China*, p. 162.

slavery, thus working toward equality between the sexes; greater egalitarianism in social organization, although titles and positions in the old Confucian pattern were to be maintained; and a kind of pure economic communism, in which property and income would belong to a group of twenty-five families. A common treasury, the redistribution of land, and a revival of the ancient *pao chia* organization, all reinforced this ideal of the militant farmer-citizen-soldier, and the brotherhood of man. Most of these plans never reached beyond the paper stage, and they were a strange

Tzu Hsi, The Empress Dowager, as a Young Woman

mixture of religious and secular, western and ancient Chinese. They had the zeal and the puritanical utopianism often associated with new dynastic movements, but their zeal reached over into fanaticism and their puritanism into assassination.

A combination of factors finally defeated them: jealousy and feuds among the Taiping leaders, especially between Hung and a second leader, Yang Hsiu-ch'ing; the failure of the bureaucrats to support those who, in attacking Confucianism, were threatening

the native philosophy as well as the foreign dynasty; the Taipings'
failure to link up with other anti-Manchu elements in China, such
as the Nien rebels to the north, the Triad Society to the south, and
the foreign powers in the treaty ports; a change of Manchu leadership in 1861, when the Hsien-feng Emperor died, replaced by
Prince Kung and the Empress Dowager Tzu Hsi, who were more
willing to cooperate with westerners and to strengthen provincial
military commanders; and finally a brilliant scholar-general,
Tseng Kuo-fan, who, accepting a small amount of western
mercenary help (led first by F.T. Ward of Salem, Massachusetts,
and later by an Englishman, "Chinese" Gordon), was able to
build up various provincial armies, finance and supply them, and
lead them to a decisive victory over the Taipings in 1864.

Hung's reputed end was dramatic. After committing suicide by
swallowing gold coins, he was buried before Nanking was taken,
but later his body was disinterred and his severed head was taken
to the gloating Empress Dowager in Peking. Thus the Manchus,
now led by a beautiful and ruthless Empress, limped into the second half of the nineteenth century.

The Taiping Program

We brothers and sisters, enjoying today the greatest mercy of our Heavenly Father, have become as one family and are able to enjoy true blessings; each of us must always be thankful. Speaking in terms of our ordinary human feelings, it is true that each has his own parents and there must be a distinction in family names; it is also true that as each has his own household, there must be a distinction between this boundary and that boundary. Yet we must know that the ten thousand names derive from the one name, and the one name from one ancestor. Thus our origins are not different. Since our Heavenly Father gave us birth and nourishment, we are of one form though of separate bodies, and we breathe the same air though in different places. This is why we say: "All are brothers within the four seas." Now, basking in the profound mercy of Heaven, we are of one family. Brothers and sisters are all of the same parentage; as all are born of one Spiritual Father, why should there be the distinctions of "you and I," or "others and ourselves"? When there is clothing, let all wear it; when there is food, let all eat of it. When someone is ill, others should ask a doctor to treat him and take care of his medicine. We must treat parentless boys and girls and persons of advanced age with more care, bathing them and washing and changing their clothes. Thus we will not lose the idea of sharing joys and sorrows, as well as mutual concern over pain and illness. Safety for the old, sympathy for the young, and compassion for the orphaned, all emerge from the Eastern King's understanding of our Heavenly Father's love for the living and from the Heavenly King's treating all as brothers and fellow beings.

As for (maintaining) our brothers' peace in the camps, everyone must be kind, industrious, and careful. When the skies are clear the soldiers should be drilled, and when it rains the heavenly books should be read, clearly expounded and mutually discussed, so that everybody will know the nature of Heaven and forever abide by the true Way. If the demons advance, at the first beat of the signal drums, everyone must hurriedly arm himself with gun, sword, or spear, and hasten to the palace to receive orders. In charging forward, each must strive to be in the front, fearing to be left behind, and none must shirk responsibilities. Thus will we be of one virtue and of one heart. Even if there are a million demons, they will not be hard to exterminate instantly.

We brothers, our minds having been awakened by our Heavenly

Father, joined the camp in the earlier days to support our Sovereign, many bringing parents, wives, uncles, brothers, and whole families. It is a matter of course that we should attend to our parents and look after our wives and children, but when one first creates a new rule, the state must come first and the family last, public interests first and private interests last. Moreover, as it is advisable to avoid suspicion (of improper conduct) between the inner (female) and the outer (male) and to distinguish between male and female, so men must have male quarters and women must have female quarters; only thus can we be dignified and avoid confusion. There must be no common mixing of the male and female groups, which would cause debauchery and violation of Heaven's commandments. Although to pay respects to parents and to visit wives and children occasionally are in keeping with human nature and not prohibited, yet it is only proper to converse before the door, stand few steps apart and speak in a loud voice; one must not enter the sisters' camp or permit the mixing of men and women. Only thus, by complying with rules and commands, can we become sons and daughters of Heaven.

At the present time, the remaining demons have not yet been completely exterminated and the time for the reunion of families has not yet arrived. We younger brothers and sisters must be firm and patient to the end, and with united strength and a single heart we must uphold God's principles and wipe out the demons immediately. With peace and unity achieved, then our Heavenly Father, displaying his mercy, will reward us according to our merits. Wealth, nobility, and renown will then enable us brothers to celebrate the reunion of our families and enjoy the harmonious relations of husband and wife. Oh, how wonderful that will be! The task of a thousand times ten thousand years also lies in this; the happiness and emoluments of a thousand times ten thousand years also lie in this; we certainly must not abandon it in one day.

Excerpts are from Wm. Theodore deBary, Ed., *Sources of Chinese Tradition,* (Columbia University Press, New York, 1960), pp. 702-704.

Description of the Chinese Rebels by a Foreigner

A noisy particoloured crowd, jostling each other into the water in their anxiety to inspect us, received us as we stepped on shore. We were surrounded by a mob of these long-haired, long-robed ragamuffins as we walked into the fort through the wretched gateway which served as its principal entrance, and, passing along a narrow, half-ruined street, were ushered into a dilapidated yamen in a state of repair. Strains of discordant music announced our approach to the high dignitary within, whom we found seated in solemn state behind a high table or altar, upon which stood two open carved jars like wine coolers, of silver or imitation silver, which contained long thin slips of wood covered with Chinese characters. The chamber was a small, square apartment, hung with scrolls of yellow silk, covered with texts and mottoes in Chinese, belonging, apparently, as much to Confucianism as to Christianity; and the presiding genius himself was a stout, sensual-looking man, with a keen eye, and an intelligent but bad cast of countenance. He was dressed in a robe of yellow silk which fell from his neck to his heels, and was devoid of ornament; round his head was wrapped an orange-coloured handkerchief, in the centre of which, above the forehead, was fastened a single piece of jade, mounted in a gold setting. His long hair was collected in a bag, and hung in the nape of his neck, as though an imitation of the fashion prevalent among English young ladies of the present day.

Bowing to us slightly as we entered, How – for so was this great man called – beckoned us to chairs, the mob by which we had been followed crowding unceremoniously into the small apartment. Not the smallest respect was shown by the insubordinate rabble to their leader, who strove in vain to keep them from pressing round, much to the disparagement of the dignified manner which he evidently desired to maintain in our presence, and by which he hoped to impress us with a due sense of his rank and importance. The odour of garlic which pervaded his undisciplined retainers, their boisterous and noisy manner and filthy aspect, rendered our audience by no means so agreeable as it might otherwise have been. A perfect equality seemed to reign, or rather an absolute confusion of ranks and persons, well dressed and ragged, old and young, thronged impetuously into the little room. It struck me, however, that the young predominated: many of these had been

61

rebels all their lives, and had no tails, but generally the tail was wrapped round the long tangled hair.

How told us that to his functions of commander and judge he united those of high priest. The thin slips of wood in the silver vases were inscribed with various punishments, and the form of sentencing consisted in his selecting and throwing to the criminal the punishment to which he was condemned . . .

The leaders were Canton men of the worst description. Drunkenness and opium-smoking were prevalent vices, as one of their number, who spoke Cantonese English, and was evidently a blackguard of the first water, unhesitatingly admitted. In the original code promulgated by T'ai P'ing, opium-smoking was punishable by death. One of the first questions we were asked by How was, "What have you got to sell?" They were evidently skeptical when we denied that we were traders, and How recurred to the subject before we left him. He had been a merchant in a small way at Canton.

We now proceeded to the exploration of the surrounding streets, and . . . were accompanied on our rambles by a crowd, with the more intelligent of whom Mr. Wade got into conversation upon religious subjects; but their theology was of the vaguest description, and did not prevent them from using the foulest language to each other. We saw very few women, and they were evidently all from the north, probably captured on some of their raids in that direction.

From a description supplied by a western traveller, Lawrence Oliphant, in 1858, and quoted by Roger Pelissier in *The Awakening of China 1793-1949*, (G. P. Putnam's Sons, New York, 1966), pp. 150-151.

5

Decline of a Dynasty

Having survived its greatest challenges so far in the 1850's and 1860's, the Manchu dynasty went on to enjoy a modest revival. In their early years the leadership of Prince Kung and the Empress Dowager Tzu Hsi was realistic and strong, a relief from the self-absorbed Hsien-feng Emperor. They had great faith in Tseng Kuo-fan, the "Confucian General" much admired in his own time and since, and in his energetic colleague Li Hung-chang. Tseng and Li engineered a movement of "Self-Strengthening," which aimed at responding just enough to the Western challenge to avoid confrontations which China would surely lose, but without sacrificing any of China's essential nature in the process. The old tribute days were over, but Chinese leaders were still convinced of her essential superiority. The explanation Tseng gave for self-strengthening was:

"Chinese learning for the fundamental structure;
Western learning for practical use."

In a way it was a deeply conservative movement, yet it led to many needed reforms. Tseng and his colleagues revived the examination system, so that it was less corrupt and a better indicator of the Confucian moral excellence which Tseng himself displayed. They discovered new sources of taxation on commerce to replace the old sources which were no longer effective, and in certain areas of the Empire they were able to regularize taxation and reduce the amount of the squeeze. Li Hung-chang was an ardent promoter of industrialization for China, under a form of organization which he called "Official Supervision and Merchant Management." This was an updated version of the old salt monopoly, and used government expertise and a certain amount of money (although most of the money needed came from private sources attracted by the prestige of government interest) in order to develop new industries. The most outstanding of these industries were the building of steamships, coal mines, railroads and cotton mills. For a few years, Chinese activity in those areas was impressive, the Chinese even winning back the Yangtze River carrying trade from the British and the Americans. But "official supervision" of industrial projects came to mean official strangulation as well as lots of official squeeze. Profits which could have been used to develop even more industries were drained off by the government to meet other expenses. And Li Hung-chang, by becoming very wealthy from his various enterprises, certainly set a bad example for capitalism. But the literati didn't even need bad examples to be distrustful.

Another problem arose when the industrialists tried to move into the countryside. "Feng-shui," translated as "the winds and waters of a place," were what made the place special, even sacred, both to living men and to their ancestors. The "feng-shui" represented the past and present harmony between man and nature, which would be lost if there was too much tampering. Digging mines, laying railroad track, stringing telegraph wires, crucial though they are to economic development, are destructive to the feelings of peace and beauty that a place can give to a person. Many riots actually occurred over the disrupting of "feng-shui," which showed how essentially conservative the Chinese were, and unready for the supposed benefits of modernization which the self-strengtheners and the westerners were pressing on them.

The "feng-shui" were not the only factors in the slow growth of modern transportation or communication in China. The railroads represented foreign influence and threat, especially in northern Manchuria where the Russians used the railroad which they built to Vladivostok as a way to control the region. Money was hard to raise, technology was western and thus either unknown or offensive to many of China's brightest young minds, and western competition within China itself undermined many of China's own "infant industries." Furthermore, many Chinese, looking at their river system which had been serving the purpose of transportation for hundreds of years, didn't feel the need for a quicker or more direct route.

Tseng was an inspiring leader, a Confucian who was able to handle the idea that there were many kinds of knowledge in the world and that the Chinese had better know them all. But the Chinese literati as a whole were a very conservative group. They had studied for years; they had made a considerable investment of their lives in one form of knowledge, the Chinese classics; and they felt tremendously threatened by any other. Furthermore, modernization is such an enormous and dislocating project that one has to be totally committed to it even to start. To build an arsenal one must read technical books, which leads to language study, which might lead to foreign travel — and so an endless process begins.

Furthermore, the few brave Chinese, like Yung Wing, who had studied abroad and even graduated from Yale University, found it hard to make places for themselves when they returned to China eager to put their exciting new knowledge to China's use.

During the first few years after the Arrow War the western nations were prepared to stand by the Manchu throne as the best arrangement which they could make in China. Their view of the fanaticism of the Taipings had scared them, and they even helped to a certain extent in putting the rebellion down. The British, who were now trading in China more than ever, and who had a number of officials who understood the Chinese position as well as their own, led the other western nations in this "cooperative policy."

Many feelings of hostility, however, were never far below the surface. In 1870 the Tientsin Massacre inspired them again, and also showed the extent to which the western nations were willing to violate China's sovereignty in order to defend their own nationals in China. The Tientsin Massacre occurred because of the practice of the French nuns in the Tientsin Cathedral of welcoming young Chinese babies and children for whom their Chinese parents did not feel they could care. The nuns were so horrified by tales of infanticide and of child neglect that they even offered to pay a nominal sum to anyone who brought in a child. This nominal sum seemed like a lot of money to the Chinese, who immediately grew very suspicious. They heard stories of kidnapping to gain the reward. The nuns' big black robes, especially when they were energetically taking care of the children, flew about and reminded the Chinese of enormous birds. Celibacy seemed an unrealistic way of life. Who were these women and why in the world had they gone so far from their homes to do what they did? More and more Chinese began to believe that the nuns must be hiding something, must be up to no good in that cathedral. After a while, many were convinced that the nuns were feasting on the eyes, hearts and livers of the little Chinese children who were being presented to them. How else could one explain their strange behavior?

In June a crowd gathered, filled with the local gentry as well as the local hotheads, demanding that the nuns give up the children. The French consul over-reacted; he demanded that the crowd disperse, and when it didn't, he shot at the Magistrate. He missed, but the crowd, now totally enraged, did not. He was literally torn apart, and others were killed too: nuns, priests, and Chinese servants in the cathedral. Much property was destroyed as well.

The French immediately sent gunboats to Tientsin, and demanded restitution. The aging Tseng Kuo-fan looked into the affair with his customary judiciousness, and presented the facts as he saw them to both the Chinese and the French. Neither side was satisfied. There was no war over the incident, mostly because the French were busy in Europe at the time. But the hopeful first days of Sino-western cooperation in "self-strengthening" were over, to be replaced by a more overt suspiciousness. Chinese patriots began to speak about how the ordinary Chinese citizen could take only so much from the westerners, and that at a certain point his anger would erupt and he would defend himself. From then on, those who were resisting change were also waiting for that point.

Modernization might have been carried off anyway, as it was in Japan in the face of a far-from-enthusiastic populace, if Tzu Hsi had really been behind it. She was a difficult and vacillating woman, but devoted to the interests of China as she saw them. Able, intelligent, and strong at a time when China needed firm leadership, fiercely proud and pleasure-loving, she was afraid of foreigners and of anyone else who might threaten her precarious position on the Dragon Throne. She had been a concubine, and reached power by a combination of factors: her beauty and personal attraction for the Hsien-feng Emperor, her motherhood of the only heir, and the personal loyalty which she was able to muster from Prince Kung, brother of the Hsien-feng Emperor, the Manchu bannerman soldier Jung-lu, and certain palace eunuchs during the chaotic period just after the burning of the summer palace and the death of the Emperor.

She was personally dominant over her son all through his childhood. When he grew up, he took over many of his duties, with her help and advice, but then he mysteriously died (some say the Empress had introduced him to a dissipating lifestyle to encourage such an outcome) and equally mysteriously, his young and pregnant wife committed suicide. Tzu Hsi then put her own nephew, who was only marginally related to the ruling line, on the throne, and enjoyed another long spell as Empress Dowager.

Many of the political and military officials near the top owed their appointments to her. She was also adept at counter-balancing the new regional interests being built up by the "self-strengtheners" and the traditional central dynastic power. The Chinese people, awed by her power, beauty and the sheer length of her tenure, ended up by affectionately calling her the "Old Buddha". As one observer put it:

> For thirty-seven years . . . she ruled the Palace and those
> nearest her with virtually absolute power, and for eleven years

she ruled indirectly — a total of forty-eight years. Her outstanding endowments were an unquenchable ambition, a love of power, a love of money, and a physical vitality which almost never failed. She knew both the strength and weaknesses of men in high places; tactfully she used their talents to carry out great policies, and did not scruple to take advantage of their foibles for ends both selfish and cruel. She was superstitious, but in matters of policy was realistic. Considering her limited advantages, she gained a broad view of Chinese literature and a good working knowledge of the Chinese documentary style. She was interested in music and art, and the theatre owed much to her patronage. Her calligraphy was better than average and she could also paint.*

"Progress" could only be seen by Tzu Hsi and much of the bureaucracy against the much more important backdrop of the retention of their own power. By the 1880's and early 1890's, the momentum behind modernization had been killed by all of these factors.

In 1895, China's weakness was revealed for all the world to see when it went to war with the aggressive and modernized Japan over Korea. Korea had been under Chinese sway for centuries, but the new balance of power in the Far East threatened China's claim that it had suzerainty over it. Although China was by far the larger nation, and even had more warships, they were older and of inferior quality. The Empress Dowager had been given the money by her top officials to modernize her navy, but had used the money instead to build a beautiful marble ferryboat at the Summer Palace! China was defeated on the land, too, and at the end of the war Japan dominated Korea and was even eyeing Manchuria.

When Li Hung-chang went to Japan to negotiate a treaty of peace, he managed to get an advantage out of the fact that he was shot at by a fanatical Japanese patriot. The bullet hit just below the eye; and after he was bandaged, the negotiations proceeded, embarrassing the Japanese negotiator, Ito. There is a story that Ito turned to Li Hung-chang at some point in the negotiations and said to him, "Ten years ago at Tientsin I talked with you about reform. Why is it that up to now not a single thing has been changed or reformed?" To which Li answered, "Affairs in my country have been so confined by tradition."**

*Arthur W. Hummel, ed., *Eminent Chinese of the Ch'ing Period,* (1644-1912), 2 vols., (Washington, D.C., 1943), 1:300.

**Orville Schell and Joseph Esherick, *Modern China: The Making of a New Society from 1839 to the Present,* (New York, 1972), p. 39.

Modern Tourists on the Empress Dowager's Ferry Boat at the
Summer Palace

Now the Japanese had to be added to the list of foreigners pressing China for concessions. It was all the more humiliating for the
Chinese, who called the Japanese "robber-dwarfs" and who had
always assumed a superiority, if not toward the West lately, at
least toward other Asians. In the Treaty of Shimonoseki, the

Chinese gave up claims to Formosa, the Pescadores, and the Liaotung Peninsula. They agreed that Korea would be independent, which really meant that it would be open to domination by Japan, and they paid an indemnity, which they could ill afford to do. Basically, all China's tariffs for some time to come were now earmarked for Japan.

The most disastrous effects of the Sino-Japanese War, however, were yet to come. Full of imperialistic fervor after colonizing Africa, the western powers now turned to an obviously weak China ready, as one observer put it, to "carve it up like a melon." Different areas, while not militarily occupied or politically governed, and whose boundaries were somewhat fuzzy, were nevertheless designated as "spheres of influence" for Great Britain, France, Russia and Germany. The Russians' sphere was in the north, especially in Manchuria, the Germans were in the coal-rich Shantung peninsula, the British kept a grip on the Yangtze Basin, as well as the Hong Kong-Kowloon area, and the French moved into the south, to be near their new colony of Indochina. The United States, interested in open trade rather than industrial development far from home, did not join the scramble for a sphere. Its purity as a non-imperialist, celebrated then and since, was not complete, however, as in 1899 it unsuccessfully tried to lease a naval base. Within these "spheres" all industrial, trade and banking decisions, and not a few political ones, could be made only with the approval of the European nation dominant in the area. Strong military and naval bases were built within the spheres, and much mining and railroad development was planned, often with the help of a well-placed bribe or two.

Reaction to both the defeat by Japan and the "spheres" was harsh within China. Clandestine "secret societies" rose sharply in both number and potential violence. These secret societies were mostly anti-foreign and deeply conservative, but they were also increasingly anti-Manchu. As a young man, for example, Sun Yat-sen turned against the Manchus after the French had taken Indochina, and the Manchus had not stopped them. He decided then that a foreign dynasty should not be allowed to preside over the dismemberment of the Chinese Empire.

Besides secret societies, "study societies" were formed which investigated aspects of China which needed reforms, such as the post office, law, and examination system, and others. In addition to accepting the reality of the western and Japanese threat, these reformers, whose leaders were K'ang Yu-wei and Liang Ch'i-ch'ao, used their base in the scholar gentry to reinterpret the classics, and they discovered that Confucius was really the greatest reformer of them all.

Through their positions as advisors to the young Kuang-Hsu Emperor, Tzu Hsi's nephew (she had been in retirement since 1889), K'ang and Liang gained his support and in 1898 they effected the famous Hundred Days of Reform. More than forty reform edicts were issued during this period, concerning all kinds of matters from education to agriculture, military modernization, commercial development and the reform of China's laws so that the hated onus of extraterritoriality might be ended. Many of the Manchus' favorite sinecure posts were abolished by the young Chinese reformers. But few of the reforms were carried out, as the bureaucrats waited to see what the "Old Buddha" would do. Sure enough, she rose to the bait, seized and virtually imprisoned the Emperor,* and called off nearly all of the reforms. K'ang and Liang escaped to Japan in time, but six other reformers were executed.

Although K'ang and Liang seemed very radical to the Empress, the fact that they were still loyal to the Ch'ing dynasty and the imperial system meant that they actually were not really extreme. Their place as dissenters was taken by republicans, by secret society members, by those who were not content with gradualism and were more prone to the use of violence.

The Boxers were among these dissenters. The members of this secret society, known as the Order of Righteous and Harmonious Fists, practiced their military exercises so diligently, combining them with Taoist sayings and the worship of belligerent Chinese heroes, that they came to believe that they would be invulnerable to the bullets of their enemies. They had started as an anti-dynastic group, but during 1899 they shifted their animosity from the Ch'ing dynasty to the westerners, especially to Christians, and to anyone who had become too close to the westerners, such as Chinese Christians. It was these Chinese Christians whom the Boxers began killing in northern Chinese villages and towns during late 1899 and early 1900. Conditions in these towns were bleak anyway. The imminent breakup of China was feared, and there was poverty and banditry everywhere. The Boxers' anger at the foreigners was but a mirror of the Empress Dowager's own feelings, and she said, "China is weak; the only thing we can depend on is the hearts of the people. If we lose them, how can we main-

---

*He lived in a little castle on an island in the lake at the Summer Palace for most of the rest of his life.

tain our country?''* Tzu Hsi knew that the Boxers might easily turn against the dynasty and that many of her officials regarded them as the true Chinese voice which would not put up with foreign exploitation any longer. She knew that her imperial armies were refusing to fight the Boxers, preferring to harry foreigners. She had, in addition, been convinced by the Manchu princes, increasingly her only informants, that the Boxers really *were* invincible, that foreign bullets hit their chests and just as promptly bounced right off again.

Thus it was that the court made only the most minimal effort to control the Boxer threat, and in some areas, namely Shansi and Shantung provinces, local gentry and bureaucrats seemed actually to support the dissenters. In June of 1900 the Boxers entered Peking. After much killing and burning, they surrounded the foreign legations and held about one thousand Europeans and three thousand Chinese Christians in siege for forty-five days. The besieged survived reasonably well, thanks to superb organization, much bravery, and the British supply of polo ponies which, alas, ended up as supper. In other areas in north China, Europeans and Chinese Christians did not fare as well and hundreds were killed in June and July, including the German Minister, Baron Clemens von Ketteler.

Meanwhile the western powers were trying to organize an expedition of 20,000 troops to march to Peking and relieve the legations. Though they met unexpectedly tough resistance from the Boxers and Imperial Troops along the railway, their biggest delays were caused by their competitiveness with each other. When they got to Peking in early August, they found that the Chinese also were divided in their aims and in their methods. Some were fighting a last-ditch effort to get rid of the foreigners in China once and for all, whereas others like the Manchu bannerman, Jung-lu, seemed more measured in their resistance. Furthermore, no Empress Dowager could be found at all. Soon the westerners learned that the Empress had decided that she wanted to take a "tour of her western provinces" and had disappeared in the direction of the northwest. Then sixty-five, she had to travel disguised in peasant clothes, her fingernails cut, hiding under the straw in the back of a simple cart. She saw first hand what kind of life was led by most of the people in China, and it made a very big impression on her.

Back in Peking, Chinese such as Li Hung-chang and Jung-lu, who were determined to try to placate the westerners, worked out the Boxer Protocol by September, 1901. The delay was caused by

*Chester C. Tan, *The Boxer Catastrophe,* (New York, 1967), p. 72.

the westerners, especially the Germans and the Russians, who were determined to get many concessions and much money out of the Chinese in revenge for all the suffering their nations had undergone. The Empress, who was in spite of all her mistakes an important symbol to the Chinese, was spared. But others who had collaborated with the Boxers lost their lives, or their jobs, or in certain areas, the right to take the official examinations. This was to punish the local gentry in those areas, essentially by denying them entrance into the scholar bureaucracy. The westerners also fortified their legations, as well as the railroad from Tientsin to Peking.

Most westerners now openly admitted that they wanted China humiliated. Besides an official apology, they also insisted that to memorialize the death of the German Minister, there be built "on the place where the murder was committed . . . a commemorative monument suitable to the rank of the deceased, bearing an inscription in the Latin, German and Chinese languages expressing the regret of the Emperor of China for the murder."*

There was, finally, the indemnity. Although the Chinese, Americans and even the French were mindful of what the Chinese *could* pay as well as what they *should* pay, the Germans, British and Russians felt that their nations should be repaid for every penny spent in the incident. The amount finally settled on was 450 million taels, or $333 million dollars, clearly out of the question for the Chinese. It was arranged that they could turn over revenues from the customs and the salt monopoly, adding to them interest charges, for the next forty years.

The Americans acted as somewhat of a brake on this scramble to dismantle what was left of China. John Hay, the American Secretary of State, declared in a major statement, the Open Door Policy, that although spheres existed in China, they should not deny trade to all nations. Later he added the statement that Chinese territorial integrity should be protected. The other nations went along with this policy, at least in their public statements, as the problems in the relief expedition had convinced them that carving up China among imperialistic powers would not be easy. Besides that, by the early twentieth century the bloom was off the rose of political imperialism, serious resistance having developed in India and other areas. In this way, slowly, the threat of outright political partition was lifted and the westerners went back to an interest in trade, missionary work, and economic development.

*Tan, *The Boxer Catastrophe,* p. 150.

Early in 1902, in spite of the vast diplomatic setback which the Boxer Protocol represented, the Empress returned from Sian in a jovial mood and promising reforms. She welcomed the foreign ministers sweetly, and invited their wives to tea. One westerner even claimed to have had an affair with her,* and although she was seventy years old at the time, it wouldn't have surprised Peking society.

The Empress Dowager Receiving Western Ladies After the Boxer
Rebellion

Her experience in western China, as well as her awareness of China's weakness, made the Empress' desire for reforms more sincere now than it had ever been. But it was too late now for reforms to do anything but weaken the dynasty. The abolition of the examination system in 1905 is an example. It weakened the

*Hugh Trevor-Roper, *Hermit of Peking: The Hidden Life of Sir Edmund Backhouse,* (New York, 1978), p. 311.

loyalty of the old Confucian scholars to the throne without creating any new body of competent government workers to take their place. Although considerable resources, including returned Boxer indemnity funds, were devoted to foreign study and the creation of a new student class, this class was still very weak. They were young, still studying; the students' experiences at home and especially abroad were unsettling to them, and there remained the principal problem of how to relate their new knowledge to the Chinese situation.

Exposure to the new learning meant exposure to constitutionalism, women's rights, perhaps even something called "democracy." Even a person such as Han Suyin's father, who was trained in Europe to be a railroad engineer, found when he returned to China that he knew too much about some things and not enough about others, and that his Belgian wife, foreign sympathies, and liberal ideas on politics all impeded his ability to do useful work in China.* On the other hand, some of the other new students were going to military academies and then working in modernized armies such as that in North China under Yuan Shih-k'ai, who inherited a position as a senior Chinese official after Li's death in 1901 and Jung-lu's in 1903. This meshing of new learning with new militarism was strange in view of the tradition of anti-militarism in China. It lent a new prestige to the military approach and was potentially dangerous, as China was soon to see.

Tzu Hsi allowed the idea of provincial assemblies to be considered, and they were planned, but they were merely "advisory," and all the discussion did was to intensify the idea of regionalization. At the same time, nationalism, the concept of a strong and effective China, unified by more than just its xenophobia and its sense of a superior culture, began to appeal to more and more people. K'ang Yu-wei and Liang Ch'i-ch'ao had stood for a strong as well as a reformed China, but they were primarily intellectuals and propagandists rather than dedicated revolutionaries.

A more vibrant leader soon emerged in Sun Yat-sen, a Cantonese with a hot temper and the capacity for total commitment. A peasant's son who had admired the Taipings as a boy, he always insisted on being Hung Hsui-Chuan when the children played games. When he grew up, besides his passion, which was sorely needed as a contrast to centuries of Confucian compassion, he had spent three years in Honolulu pursuing a western education. He was at home with westerners, which made him attractive to them,

*Han Suyin, *The Crippled Tree,* (New York, 1965).

and a good money-raiser among both them and the overseas Chinese.

Although he was trained as a western doctor, Sun was never able to make a living in China because the westerners wouldn't let him practice without a license earned in one of their nations and the Chinese were afraid of western medicine. Thus thwarted, he began the long, lonely and dangerous life of a revolutionary. He began normally enough by joining a secret society, the long-standing Triad Society, but soon he created his own. In spite of his fancy credentials of medicine and foreign study, he based his desire for an uprising on the poverty and indignity of China. "I am the son of a peasant family," he insisted, "and know about the hardships of life in agriculture."*

Sun and his cohorts made plans to capture isolated government offices, confident that such dramatic acts would spur on other Chinese to resist Manchu authority. Their first plot was intercepted, however, in 1895, and several of them were executed. Sun fled to Japan, where he cut off his queue, the single pigtail which Chinese men were invariably expected to wear to signify their loyalty to the Manchus. The queue-cutting was not, however, prompted so much by his desire to make a brave revolutionary statement as it was by his desire to change his appearance. He grew a mustache, stopped shaving his head, and was rather surprised at how Japanese he looked. He even began to wear European clothes, an odd uniform for a Chinese patriot.

For the moment isolated from China, Sun needed publicity to raise money and morale, and to make his followers' desperate acts of courage mean anything. He suspected that the Chinese government might pursue him all over the world, and he was right. In 1896, having travelled to London via Hawaii and the United States, he was held captive in the Chinese Embassy and threatened with execution. It is a matter of argument whether he had been kidnapped or had entered the Embassy incautiously in spite of his personal danger. But it is certain that his Chinese guards were jubilant. "We are going to gag you," one of them said, "and tie you up, put you in a bag, and take you to a steamer we have already chartered." If that plan failed, they threatened to kill him inside the Legation, on the grounds that "The Legation is China; we can do anything here."**

*Harold Z. Schiffirin, *Sun Yat-sen and the Origins of the Chinese Revolution,* (Berkeley, 1970), p. 63.

**Schiffirin, *Sun Yat-sen,* pp. 115-116.

Sun was to show the bravery and persistence in this episode which was part of his personality all his life. After repeated interceptions of his messages to influential British friends, he finally smuggled one out successfully, and his allies went to work. Twelve days later, his release was finally secured, all under the watchful eye of the London *Times*. Sun was not only safe; he had become a celebrity, even a hero.

Collecting support from modernizers, secret societies such as his own, the T'ung Meng Hui, overseas Chinese, returned students, intellectual leaders, and rootless military bands, Sun served as the personal focus of the anti-Manchu movement. Besides his personal magnetism, Sun had a program, called the "Three Principles of the People," in which he outlined his plans for a post-Ch'ing China. First of all, he wanted to have a strong and modern nationalism, to replace the culturalism which had made China into nothing more than what he called a "heap of loose sand." In the past, it was possible that China's decision to follow the virtue rather than the command ethic had been wise. In modern times, however, dominated by arms and imperialists, he said, "Other men are carving knife and serving dish; we are fish and meat." Second, he espoused democracy for China, but only after a period of what he called "political tutelage," during which time well-educated Chinese would be expected to ready the people for democracy. Finally, Sun advocated the improvement of the people's livelihood, through heavy government taxation of any increase in land values. The money gained from taxes would be used to promote industrialization. Although this last principle is what the Communist Chinese most favor about Sun, Sun himself felt that the application of Marx's ideas to China would be "impracticable."

Sun's ideas were sufficiently vague in their phrasing to include much that was both old and new, Chinese and western. Most of all, Sun's three principles carried much of the liveliness and compassion of his own personality. It was a revolutionary document which at the same time gave him the air of a statesman.

This combination of private plotting and public statements came to an end sooner than one might have thought. The "Old Buddha" died in 1908; within hours the Kuang-hsu Emperor had died as well, and a three-year old was named as regent. This guaranteed not only another weak successor, but that a crowd of ill-informed and anti-reform Manchu princes would run nothing but a holding operation.

The pattern of local uprisings began to step up: Hunan, Canton, and finally Wuchang, in Hupei, on the tenth of October, since celebrated as the "Double Ten," in 1911. At that point Sun Yat-sen had been officially exiled from China for many years, although he had been able to get into China under various disguises for brief stays when he had met and inspired several major revolutionaries, such as Huang Hsing from Hunan province. At the time of the Double Ten, Sun was in the United States seeking funds. He read about the revolution in a Denver newspaper while he was sitting in a coffee shop one morning ordering his breakfast. He couldn't claim to have masterminded the rebellion, but it went as he had planned it, in a chain reaction. Anti-Manchu demonstrations occurred in several cities, and one by one the provinces declared their independence from Manchu control. The forces behind the rebellion were the members of the provincial assemblies, secret societies, especially those influenced by Sun, and soldiers. There were only a few battles, but there were incidents and exterminations of the Manchus in several cities. The end of the dynasty came when it was forced to call on the ablest Chinese general, Yuan Shih-k'ai, who had been fired in 1909, for help. He still had vast military power based on the loyalty of the new army, and he agreed to keep order, but only if the form of government was completely changed.

Sun Yat-sen had rushed home to be made President of the Chinese Republic on January 1, 1912 in Nanking, but he soon offered to resign so that Yuan could govern the country. He felt that only Yuan had the experience and the connections, as well as the temperament, to be an administrator in a very difficult transition period. Sun expected, though, to retain much moral influence.

In February, 1912, because of Yuan's maneuverings, the Manchus formally withdrew. In a moving statement, the young Emperor acknowledged that the dynasty had lost the Mandate, and no longer enjoyed the confidence of the people. Thus ended the last of China's imperial dynasties.

Opium and the Disintegrating Chinese Family

When we had finished what they gave us we begged as before. One day as I was walking along a man called to me.

"Is not your name Ning?" I hurried along. I tucked the stick further up my sleeve. I was now in the part of the city where my people had lived. I had moved back into the home nest, but would not shame them by being known as a beggar.

"Is there not a man named Ning, called so and so?" asked the stranger. I said that I knew nothing about what he was saying. Then the man said, "I have heard of such a man bargaining to sell a child."

I was young then and had no experience. I thought, "Could he really think to sell our child?"

When I got home I asked him. He laughed and said, "They must have heard me joking one day."

I believed him. I was young and simple then. I was only twenty-two.

In the winter the rich of the city built mat sheds under which they gave out gruel to the poor. We went every day for one meal of hot gruel. We met there, for he begged in one part of the city, carrying Chinya, and I begged in another, leading Mantze.

One day when my husband handed the baby over to me as usual, saying, "Nurse her," one of the men in charge of the gruel station saw him do it.

"Is that your man?" said the man from the gruel station. I answered that he was.

"He is trying to sell the child. He tells people that her mother died last Seventh Month."

"Oh, that is the talk that he uses for begging," I said. But in my heart I wondered if it was true that he was trying to sell our child and to keep the knowledge from me.

One day, when the ground was wet with melting snow, I found that even with the three pairs of shoes my feet were not covered. The bare flesh showed through.

"You stay at home," he said, "and I will beg." He took the child in his arms as usual. "You wait at home," he said. "I will bring you food."

We waited, Mantze and I. The day passed; it got dark; and still he did not come. It was cold. I opened my clothes and took Mantze inside my garments to give her warmth, and still he did not

78

come. We lay in the dark. We had no lights that winter; we had no money for oil. I heard the watchman beating the third watch and I knew the night was half over. Still he did not come.

Then I heard him push open the door and stumble as he crossed the threshold. He was opium sodden and uncertain in his movements. I waited for him to say as usual, "Here, take the child and nurse her." But there was no word. I heard him throwing something heavily on the bed.

"Now you have knocked the breath out of the child. Give her to me."

Still he said nothing.

"What is the matter? Give me the child." And he only grunted.

"Light the lamp and I will tell you," he said.

"It is not the custom to light lamps in this house. Do you not know me or do I not know you that we must have a light to talk by to each other? Tell me." Then he struck a match and I saw that there was no child, only a bundle, a bundle of sweet potatoes.

"I have sold her."

I jumped out of bed. I had no thought left for Mantze. I seized him by the queue. I wrapped it three times around my arm. I fought him for my child. We rolled fighting on the ground.

The neighbors came and talked to pacify us.

"If the child has not left the city and we can keep hold of this one, we will find her," they said.

So we searched. The night through we searched. We went to the south city through the Drum Tower and back to the examination halls. We walked a great circle inside the city, and always I walked with my hands on his queue. He could not get away.

We found a house. The father of the child knocked. Some men came to the door. It was the house of dealers who buy up girls and sell them to brothels in other cities. Their trade is illegal, and if they are caught they are put in prison and punished. They dared not let me make a noise. I had but to cry aloud and the neighbors would be there. So the dealer in little girls said soft words. My neighbors said, "What he says, he will do. Now that we have him we will find the child." But the child was not in that house.

"Take me to my child," I demanded. The man promised. So again we started out in the night, walking and stumbling through the streets. Then one of my neighbors who had more power to plan than the others said, "Why do you still hold on to him? He is now useless." I still had my arm twisted in my husband's queue. "Hold on to that one so he does not run away. He it is that knows where the child is."

So I let go of my husband's queue and in one jump was beside the man and had seized him by the slack of his coat. "Why do you seize me?" he said.

"So that you will not run away and I lose my child again." My husband was gone into the night, and still we walked. We came to the entrance of a narrow street.

"You stay here," said the man, "I will go in and call them."

"No," said I. "Where you go, I go. What kind of a place is this that I cannot go with you?"

And when he said that it was a residence, I said, "A residence! If you, a man, can go, surely I, a woman can do so. If it was a bachelor's lair I still would go in to find my child." I held onto him by the slack of his coat as we went down the narrow street to a gate. He knocked and still I held to him.

The man who opened it held the two parts of the gate together with his hands to prevent anyone going in. But I ducked under his arm before he could stop me and ran into the passage. I went through the courts, calling, "Chinya, Chinya." The child heard my voice and knew me and answered, and so I found her. The woman of the house tried to hide the child behind her wide sleeves, but I pushed her aside and took the child into my arms. The man barred the door and said that I could not leave.

"Then," I said, "I will stay here. My child is in my bosom. Mother and child, we will die here together." I sat on the floor with my child in my arms.

The neighbors gathered and talked. A child, they said, could not be sold without the mother's consent. He had, they said, got another five hundred cash from them by saying that I had not at first consented. They had first paid him three thousand. He had sold my child for a mere three thousand and five hundred cash.

They tried to frighten me. They said they would sell us both to get their money back. I was young then, and salable. But I said, "No. I have another child at home. I must go to that child also." The neighbors all began to talk and said that I had another child and that I must go home to her, and the dealers talked of their money they they must have back.

"You stay here until we go and get the money back," they said. But at last we all started out together. I was carrying the child and they came along to get their money. They lighted a lantern and let it shine under my feet.

Then a neighbor who thought more quickly than others said, "It is cold tonight and the way is long. We have walked far. Let me carry the child."

I said that I was well and strong and could carry her myself.

But again she said, "My coat is bigger than yours. I can carry the child inside and protect her from the cold." So I gave the child to her. She walked ahead, and gradually as they lighted the way for me she disappeared into the night. When we got home she was there with the child, but my old opium sot was gone. She knew that he would have spent all the money and would have been unable to pay, and that when they had found this out they would have taken him out and beaten him. So she had gone ahead and warned him and he had slipped away into the night. And she also had the child safely at home.

So that passed over.

He promised not to sell her again and I believed him.

The old people tell us that her husband is more important to a woman than her parents. A woman is with her parents only part of her life, they say, but she is with her husband forever. He also feels that he is the most important. If a wife is not good to her husband, there is retribution in heaven.

My husband would sit on the k'ang with his legs drawn up under his chin and his head hanging. He would raise his head suddenly and peer at me from under his lids.

"Ha! Why don't you make a plan? Why don't you think of a way for us to eat?"

I would answer, "What can I do? My family have no money. I know no one."

Then, at last, he would get up and go out to beg. People urged me to leave him and follow another man, to become a thief or a prostitute. But my parents had left me a good name, though they had left me nothing else. I could not spoil that for them.

In those years it was not as it is now. There was no freedom then for women. I stayed with him.

For another year we lived, begging and eating gruel from the public kitchen.

The father of my children was good for a while, and I thought he had learned his lesson. He promised never to sell the child again and I believed him. Then one day he sold her again and I could not get her back that time.

My little daughter was four when her father sold her the second time. When he came home without her I knew what he had done. I said that I would hang myself and that I would hang Mantze, and that we, mother and child, should die together. I rolled on the ground in my agony, in my anger, and my pain. He was frightened and said that there was no need to hang myself. He took me to the family to whom he had sold her.

It was the family of an official who had two wives. The first wife had many children but the second had none. She had been a prostitute but she was a good woman. It was she who had bought my child. She came out into the court to see me and she said many words. She said, "How can you, by begging, support two children? Your man is no good, you know that. I will not treat your child as a slave girl. I will treat her as my child. Is she not better off with me than with you? If you take her back will he not sell her again? Also you may come to see her when you like."

I knew that her words were true so I went away.

He sold her for three thousand five hundred cash the first time. I do not know for how much he sold her this second time.

Many times I went to see my little daughter and I saw that they treated her well.

They left P'englai when she was seven and I did not hear from them again until my granddaughter was half grown. Then I heard that they had done well by her. They had brought her up as a daughter, and taught her to do fine embroidery and married her to a young fruit merchant. She was well treated in the family but I never saw her again.

But because he sold her, I left my husband. I took Mantze and went away. I told him that he could live his life and that I would live mine. He lived in the house I had leased but I did not go home. When the lease was up I let it go. I let him live where he would. He lived from one opium den to another. I taught my daughter Mantze to run at the sight of him and to hide. What if he sold her also? I would not live with him.

The life of the beggar is not the hardest one. There is freedom. Today perhaps there is not enough to eat, but tomorrow there will be more. There is no face to keep up. Each day is eaten what has been begged that day. The sights of the city are free for the beggars. The temple fairs with their merrymaking crowds, the candy sticks with fluttering pennants, the whirligigs spreading noise and the colors of the rainbow in the air, women dressed in gay colors, the incense burning before the shrines and piling up in the iron pots, the flames leaping high, are harvest time for the beggars. There is drama on the open-air stage. No lady can get as close to the stage as a beggar. The ladies have their dignity to maintain and must sit in a closed cart or on the edge of the throng in tea booths. No woman but a beggar woman could see the magistrate in his embroidered ceremonial robes ride to the temples to offer sacrifice at the altars of the city in the times of festival.

At noon the beggars come to the gruel kitchen where all the

other beggars have gathered, and find human companionship. There is warm food, pleasantry, and the close feel of people around. There is no future but there is no worry. An old proverb says, "Two years of begging and one will not change places with the district magistrate." All this if a beggar is not sick.

But I was through with begging. For a year I had begged for my food but had lived in my own home. Now I could not live in my home and must "come out," even though women of my family had never "come out" before.

Ida Pruitt, *A Daughter of Han*, pp. 66-73.

The Three Principles of the People by Sun Yat Sen

On Nationalism:

For the most part the four hundred million Chinese can be spoken of as completely Han Chinese. With common customs and habits, we are completely of one race. But in the world today, what position do we occupy? Compared to the other peoples of the world we have the greatest population and our civilization is four thousand years old; we should therefore be advancing in the front rank with the nations of Europe and America. But the Chinese people have only family and clan solidarity; they do not have national spirit. Therefore even though we have four hundred million people gathered together in China, in reality they are just a heap of loose sand.

Today we are the poorest and weakest nation in the world, and occupy the lowest position in international affairs. Other men are carving knife and serving dish; we are fish and meat. Our position at this time is most perilous. If we do not earnestly espouse nationalism and weld together our four hundred million people into a strong nation, there is danger of China's being lost and our people being destroyed. If we wish to avert this catastrophe, we must espouse nationalism and bring this national spirit to the salvation of the country.

On Revolution:

Revolutionary destruction and revolutionary reconstruction complement each other like the two legs of a man or the two wings of a
bird. The republic after its inauguration weathered the storm of extraordinary destruction. This, however, was not followed by extraordinary reconstruction. A vicious cycle of civil wars has consequently arisen. The nation is on the descendant like a stream flow-
ing downward. The tyranny of the landlords together with the sinister maneuvers of the unscrupulous politicians is beyond control . . .

As a schoolboy must have good teachers and helpful friends, so
the Chinese people, being for the first time under republican rule,
must have a far-sighted revolutionary government for their training. This calls for the period of political tutelage, which is a
necessary transitional stage from monarchy to republicanism.
Without this, disorder will be unavoidable.

We cannot decide whether an idea is good or not without seeing
it in practice. If the idea is of practical value to us, it is good; if it is
impractical, it is bad. If it is useful to the world, it is good; if it is
not, it is no good.

On the People's Livelihood:

As soon as the landowners hear us talking about the land question and equalization of landownership, they are naturally alarmed
as capitalists are alarmed when they hear people talking about
socialism, and they want to rise up and fight it. If our landowners
were like the great landowners of Europe and had developed
tremendous power, it would be very difficult for us to solve the land
problem. But China does not have such big landowners, and the
power of the small landowners is still rather weak. If we attack the
problem now, we can solve it; but if we lose the present opportunity, we will have much more difficulty in the future . . .

What is our policy? We propose that the government shall levy a
tax proportionate to the price of the land and, if necessary, buy
back the land according to its price . . .

After the land values have been fixed we should have a regulation by law that from that year on, all increase in land value, which
in other countries means heavier taxation, shall revert to the community. This is because the increase in land value is due to improvement made by society and to the progress of industry and
commerce. China's industry and commerce have made little progress for thousands of years, so land values have scarcely changed
throughout these generations. But as soon as progress and improvement set in, as in the modern cities of China, land prices

change every day, sometimes increasing a thousandfold and even ten thousandfold. The credit for the progress and improvement belongs to the energy and enterprise of all the people. Land increment resulting from that progress and improvement should therefore revert to the community rather than to private individuals.

If we want to solve the livelihood problem in China and to "win eternal ease by one supreme effort," it will not be sufficient to depend only on the restriction of capital. The income tax levied in foreign countries is one method of regulating capital. But have these countries solved the problem of the people's livelihood?

China cannot be compared to foreign countries. It is not sufficient for us to regulate capital. Other countries are rich while China is poor; other countries have a surplus of production while China is not producing enough. So China must not only regulate private capital, but she must also develop state capital . . .

If we do not use state power to build up these enterprises (railroads, waterways, mines, manufacturing) but leave them in the hands of private Chinese or of foreign businessmen, the result will be the expansion of private capital and the emergence of a great wealthy class with the consequent inequalities in society . . .

China is now suffering from poverty, not from unequal distribution of wealth. Where there are inequalities of wealth, the methods of Marx can, of course, be used; a class war can be advocated to destroy the inequalities. But in China, where industry is not yet developed, Marx's class war and dictatorship of the proletariat are impracticable.

Sun Yat-sen, "Father of Modern China"

6

Problems for Democracy

Sun Yat-sen foresaw that democracy would be difficult to introduce into China. In the "Three Principles" he wrote of an interim period during which the government would have to raise up the people, lessen their dependence on authority, and teach them how to make and implement their own decisions. Even the utopian Sun realized that all of these processes would take time, perhaps as much as nine years, and that during this period a group of especially skillful people, in the army, politics, education and government, would have to lead the others on democracy's behalf.

Clever though he was, Sun didn't predict half of China's — or his own — troubles. Yuan Shih-k'ai, who talked like a republican in 1912, was talking like a new emperor in 1915. Yuan had been "given" power by Sun, but there were several reasons why he felt that he had also earned it on his own. As a military leader, only he could keep order. Without order, China would invite aggression from the greedy foreign powers, who, on the one hand, talked about the benefits of democracy, and yet who had bolstered up the Manchu regime at several points precisely because it was the central and autocratic power with which they had learned how to deal. This threat was not imagined by Yuan; it was real, and the Chinese could accept dictatorship far more readily than foreign domination.

Besides fear of disorder and disillusion with the Manchus, the new leaders of China had little to unite them. Some were republicans, some constitutional monarchists, some monarchists. Some had spent much time in Japan, some in western countries, and some had never left China. Some were brave enough to become commercially oriented in a country which for centuries had distrusted merchants. Some remained scholars; although in a new tradition of scholarship, they believed that it was the deepest thinkers who would be the wisest rulers. Some believed that the most basic institutions — the army, banking systems, schools — should be set up on a regional basis in order that modernization could proceed more quickly and be seen and used by the people. Others thought that the centralized ruling tradition dovetailed nicely with nationalism. The ousting of the Manchus had been almost too easy. The experience of working together, of ironing out differences, of unity under fire, was denied the victors. They had not had many adventures together, did not really know one another. Their aim accomplished, they were at a loss as to what to do with it.

At first Yuan tried to get along with Sun, at least on the surface. He appointed Sun to be director of China's railway system, and was cordial both to him and Huang Hsing when the two made a visit to Peking. But the alliance of the two men was soon ruptured over ideological differences and decisions about appointments. As early as 1913, after Yuan had fired some military leaders who were loyal to Sun, Sun found himself once again in Japan, exiled even from the new China. After that, his ability to come and go depended on the ebb and flow of Yuan's fortunes, but also on Sun's own relations with local Chinese leaders in Shanghai and Canton.

Many of the traditional sanctions for authority had been discredited and abolished, but the republicans were not able quickly enough to develop new ones. Attractive though Sun's democratic and emotional appeal might have seemed to a few, the Chinese were still a basically hierarchic and rational people. In a time of chaos, they would instinctively return to the old idea that "someone's in charge," rather than developing the capacity to take charge themselves.

Who would be in charge then? The national parliament? The provincial assemblies had met in a consultative capacity in the dying dynasty, and had had some part in the revolution; in 1910 they had also been joined together into a national legislative body. The question in 1912 was over whether the cabinet set up by Yuan Shih-k'ai would be responsible to him, the President, or to the national parliament. The provisional constitution, written by the brilliant Hunanese, Sung Chiao-jen, a protege of Huang Hsing, had proposed that the cabinet be responsible to both the President and the parliament. This led to many hassles, resignations, purges, moves and countermoves. The members of the Parliament had little money to spend, less control over the bureaucracy, and almost no experience in the political process. They represented the gentry rather than the peasants, and they had vast regional as well as ideological differences. For these reasons the Parliament was quickly discredited, both for being wordy and ineffective.

Would a political party be in charge, then? Sun's secret society, the T'ung Meng Hui, was refashioned by Sung Chiao-jen into the Kuo Min Tang. This political party, literally translated the National-People-Party, proposed to gain support by open elections instead of the traditional secret loyalty of the cliques, secret societies and study societies which had always been the basis of opposition groups in China. Yuan, however, was unable to understand or to accept opposition of any kind, however loyal and open. In spite of his technical expertise and modern trappings, he remained a very conservative leader.

The Kuo Min Tang gained a majority in the 1913 national legislature, partly because of Sung Chiao-jen's criticisms and successful electioneering, and in spite of the fact that Sung proposed that Yuan stay on as President, Yuan found the assumption that leaders above could be controlled by voters below to be terribly threatening. He successfully arranged to have Sung assassinated, which left the republicans leaderless and excessively timid, and denied China a strong, promising and genuinely democratic leader who might have changed the course of its history.

Would the new commercial interests have legitimate authority in China, if the parliament and the parties did not? They were so much the fledglings in any prestige sense and so paralyzed with fear that any disorder would lead to foreign invasion that they tended to support Yuan in spite of the offenses, the expenses and the tightened control which Yuan was gaining not only over the capital but over the provinces.

World War I lessened the threat from the western powers by absorbing them in their own problems, but the threat from Japan grew greater than ever. Many Chinese leaders had a "love/hate relationship" with Japan, looking on the one hand at its success as a powerful constitutional monarchy which had modernized and kept the West off its back. On the other hand, they feared its aggression and spurned its example. The recent Russo-Japanese war had left Japan even more cocky, and its aftermath was an even stronger Japanese encroachment on southern Manchuria. In this respect, Yuan's long-standing anti-Japanese record stood him in good stead, while Sun's record was compromised by the years he spent in Japan and the help which he had accepted from all manner of Japanese.

The situation was worsened in 1915 when Japan presented a list of "Twenty-One Demands," mainly for German-held concessions in Shantung province, but extending beyond that as well. Frantic by now, Yuan used all kinds of methods to hold the Japanese off and build up his own power — terrorism, dissolution of the parliament, bribery, news leaks, foreign loans, as well as the murder we have already reported. He even tried to set up a new dynasty with himself as Emperor in 1915, but the weakened republican movement was at least strong enough to thwart that action. Those who resisted Yuan's bid for power were helped by Chinese tradition. The Mandate of Heaven demanded a good leader and the "consent" of the governed. Yuan had been revealed as a clever maneuverer but essentially a shallow man, and he could not get support even among his own soldiers for his monarchical idea. He died disillusioned in 1916.

In the power vacuum left by his death emerged the authority which the Chinese had been searching for, but it was not centralized and it was not democratic. Although a series of "Presidents" in Peking claimed to rule all of China, real control was gained by the warlords — or rather, an alliance between the old landholding class, no longer softened by Confucian humanism, and the new military class. Both these groups were opportunists unsupported by any legitimate function except the most basic one of keeping order. From one of the most well-worked out rationales for central government which the world had ever seen, China in the late 1910's and early 1920's sank gradually into a primitive, violent, chaotic society of regional "governments," some papered over with democratic language and progressive programs, some nothing but geographic areas apathetically assenting to a "might is right" status quo.

The removal of the centralizing focus of the Mandate and even the counter-focus of the revolution meant that China was without a coherent policy in any area: culture, ethics, or politics. Without such a center, China flew apart. The regionalization of the self-strengthening movement, the provincial divisions of the armies, the varied atmospheres of each of the treaty ports and "spheres," all combined to deprive China of its traditional cultural unity. The constant flow of new ideas from abroad and the natural desire to try them out in small, controlled environments further spread the notion of localized rather than interconnected government.

This fractured government was supplied by the warlords, but at a high price for China. Many of the warlords had started as military governors under Yuan, and they used his methods.

> Their armies, newly swollen and Western-armed, using the new transport facilities of railways and river steamers, could now more easily dominate the terrain. Yet they could not create a new political order. In 1911 the revolutionists, with a party but no army, had failed to gain power. Now the warlords, with armies but no parties, were equally incapable of organizing a national government.*

*John K. Fairbank and Edwin Reischauer, *op. cit.,* p. 652.

Some of the warlords were better than others. One claimed to be a Christian and used to baptize his troops with a fire hose, as well as insisting on disciplined conduct from them at all times. Except for his soldiers, however, there was everywhere the traditional danger of looting by the various armies.

The warlords were tremendously antagonistic to one another, and the borders between them fluctuated, with the result that there was more uncertainty and bloodshed than at any other time in modern Chinese history. Roads and railroads between provinces deteriorated, or were actually destroyed by warlords to keep enemies from coming into their areas. Supplies often could not reach areas struck by famine. The number of people starving to death in China was higher at this time than at any other in history. Alliances between warlords were based on power considerations rather than other common goals and hence shifted often. As the country became more fragmented, the economy suffered, and poverty grew. Local landlords, often absentee, grew greedier than they had been in more stable and Confucius-dominated times. Having been knocked off his place near the top of the ethical ladder, the landlord both clung to his money and shed the restraint, dignity and sense of responsibility which had once governed his actions.

From hindsight now we can see that China was slipping more and more into the grip of the warlords, but many of the Chinese of the time couldn't see that, and they felt great hope. The May Fourth Movement was an example of both the optimism and despair of that era. It was named for a student demonstration on May 4, 1919, which protested the decision of the Versailles peace conference to give the concessions formerly held by the Germans to the Japanese. The students, having assembled peacefully, later grew violent and turned on the military clique which controlled Peking at the time, suspecting that it had accepted bribes from the westerners in return for still more concessions.

One of the students who participated in the demonstration described his feelings in this way:

> When the news of the Paris Peace Conference finally reached us we were greatly shocked. We at once awoke to the fact that foreign nations were still selfish and militaristic and that they were all great liars. I remember that the night of May 2nd very few of us slept. A group of my friends and I talked almost the whole night. We came to the conclusion that a greater world war would be coming sooner or later, and that this great war would be fought in the East. We had nothing to do with our Government, that we knew very well, and at the same time we

could no longer depend upon the principles of any so-called great leader like Woodrow Wilson, for example. Looking at our people and at the pitiful ignorant masses, we couldn't help but feel that we must struggle!*

Although named for these overt actions, which resulted in China's refusal to sign the Versailles Treaty, the May Fourth Movement had actually been building momentum ever since the Manchus had fled north of the Wall. The movement as a whole was centered around the universities in Peking, but it quickly spread to other cities. It was inspired by a new belief in nationalism, in the need to save China from its own inertia as well as from foreign threat. Most of the young reformers also were interested in modernization as well, and most were quite liberal, and interested in greater rights for the individual — thus quite anti-Confucian.

Students were not the only important members of the May Fourth Movement. Also included, in a rare and new alliance for China, were members of the working class and merchants. As for the laborers, the growth of Chinese industry during World War I had tremendously altered the pattern of Chinese family life. No longer was a son obliged to follow in his father's footsteps on the farm, deferring to him well into middle-age. No longer was a woman obliged to live as a semi-servant in the home of her mother-in-law. Jobs were available in the cities, which became hotbeds of anti-tradition and reform, with the quick communication and mass enthusiasm available which is denied the countryside. At that point the labor movement was not Marxist as most workers were more pleased by their opportunities than embittered by their exploitation. They were, however, politically aware and eager to take part in a "new" China.

The merchants, newly respected in this time of industrial growth, were also eager to take part in the nationalist movement, and proved to be able boycotters of Japanese goods. To the long-disparaged merchants in China, the anti-Confucian and anti-traditional aspect of the May Fourth reformers seemed to promise that at last they would have the chance at the power and prestige that merchants enjoyed in other countries.

Despite the laborers and the merchants, the movement was mainly an intellectual one, and this proved to be its downfall. The job to be done — to modernize all of China, even including the at-

*Chow Tse-tsung, *The May Fourth Movement*, (Cambridge, Massachusetts, 1960), p. 93.

titudes inside an ordinary Chinese person's head — was so enormous that it was difficult to tell where to start. Different people thought that they should start in different places. Some, like Hu Shih, a returned student from Columbia University in the United States (where he had studied under the famous philosopher of pragmatism, John Dewey), wanted to start with language reform, to make the written language simpler and clearer so that one could communicate with more people. Others, like Ts'ai Yuan-pei, Chancellor of the National University of Peking, wanted to search for a new morality which would bind China together, yet unleash it from old strait jackets like clannishness and the hierarchical family. Still others set up experiments testing out the feasibility of mass education and literacy as a basis for democracy. Many rejected Mencius' old idea that only the educated should govern, and, instead, glorified the dignity to be found in manual labor.

Mostly the various reformers put out magazines and formed societies, enjoyed the chaos and argued some more. It was heady excitement, but grew frustrating after a while as the "critical attitude" began to seem negative. Furthermore, the demonstrations quickly provoked a reaction in the militarists, who arrested large numbers of students and young intellectuals. Many, like Ts'ai and the young Ch'en Tu-hsiu, editor of the influential New Youth magazine, were exiled from Peking. They soon grew bitter and more radical. The "pai-hua" (simpler language, or, literally, white — pure — talk) movement proved to be of lasting importance, and the interests of the scholars, workers and merchants remained nationalistic and in common. But China's flirtation with an understanding of individuality and freedom of thought remained tentative and inconclusive.

Indeed, idealists like Sun Yat-sen grew disillusioned, not only with China, but with democracy. It began to seem too talkative and inefficient for a country as backward and poor as China. After futile efforts to influence various warlords and cliques, Sun went underground again. He returned to his old military and secretive approach, and to the conviction that violent revolution, not gradual tutelage, would be China's only salvation. Working again in Canton where he had a shaky alliance with the local warlord, he grew to admire Russia's Bolshevik revolution, then only a few years old, with its promises of rapid modernization and social equality, two items which were high on Sun's own list of priorities for China. Furthermore, Lenin, the major Bolshevik leader, claimed that capitalism led naturally to imperialism because of its need for control over resources and markets. As a good communist, therefore, Lenin renounced the imperialism in Russia's past, and even gave up the Tsar's claims in China. Cynics might say that he did so out of weakness rather than altruism or consistent policy, but to many Chinese in the early 1920's, the important part was that he did it.

"Party dictatorship" — government by a small group of people held together by a common ideology who keep tabs on each other and occasionally explain themselves to the people — also began to sound feasible and attractive to Sun Yat-sen. He felt that it might work in China, might be the instrument for the recapture of his country from the landlords and the westerners, and then for China's modernization. Sun was not a Marxist theoretically, nor did he believe that communism would work in China, a position he stated openly in 1923 when he joined the Comintern, the communist international group. The Russians, as well as their allies, the tiny Chinese Communist Party, accepted his joining on that basis. But they needed each other: he needed their support and they needed a man of his vitality and prestige to ally with during a quiet period when they were gaining strength and working underground.

Besides their need for each other, the Kuo Min Tang, the Chinese Communists and the Comintern all had several enemies in common: western bankers, traders and industrialists in China who were not only undermining Chinese industry but working outside Chinese jurisdiction; warlords, fighting with each other, terrorizing and impoverishing the people; and the liberals and democrats like Hu Shih who persisted in thinking that democracy, nonviolently and gradually arrived at, might actually work in China.

To Sun and the people around him, these liberals didn't seem tough-minded enough. They saw China at the lowest ebb of her fortunes, lower even than during the Manchus' last years. They felt that they lived in crucial times, demanding radical reactions. And so they rejected the Confucian tradition of rationality and victory-through-assimilation, and prepared themselves for another violent upheaval.

Travel in Warlord-Dominated China

Honanfu was an easy journey by train. There, thanks to Gilbert's introduction, we were able to make an appointment with Field Marshal Wu Pei Fu, whose headquarters were four miles west of the Honanfu railway station. I was much interested to have the chance to meet perhaps the greatest of China's "super-Tuchuns," (warlords) the man who had sent General Chang Tso Lin packing to Manchuria the year before, and who now ruled western China with an iron fist. Headquarters proved to be an enormous park approached by splendid roads, on which the soldiers were labouring as we came up. Plantations of young trees, fed by irrigation ditches, stretched on either side of the way, and there were immense fields of fodder corn and garden truck as orderly as an Ohio farm.

A beautiful young secretary received us in a simply furnished room hung with maps stuck with coloured pins. His white gown of silk shone immaculate among the gray uniforms, and his delicately manicured hands were pretty as any girl's. The English that he spoke, though acquired entirely at St. John's University in Shanghai, was as immaculate as his person. The general was busy but would soon receive us.

When the great man did come in, with hurried step, it was not the burly figure that I had expected. He was slight and bird-like with an unwrinkled brow, grave but not troubled. Before him lay a pile of letters which, with an apology, he unrolled and scanned as he listened while our Wang and his own secretary told him that we were simple scholars desiring to pass to the west and anxious to know from him if the roads were safe. He promptly assured us that if they weren't they could be made so, and promised a guard, explaining that the bandits were the care of the provincial officials and that he never had attempted to rid the country of them. When we said that we had hoped to go on without a guard and did not wish to appear as rich official personages, he waved our objections aside and said that ten men would be with us as far as the borders of Shensi Province. Still opening letters and occasionally signing a document or giving a short order over his shoulder to his orderly, he talked about archaeology and about paintings, getting up to point out a picture in gray ink which hung on the wall. It showed a dead plum tree stump from which a few live switches in bud had sprung up. This he said he loved, because it was the symbol of New China. Near by it, in a box of precious wood, was kept an ancient jade gong of crescent shape which gave forth a splendid deep tone when he struck it with a tiny hammer.

Much as I longed to draw him out on the subject of politics and the presidential election which was then hanging in the balance, our role was to be innocent of such things and to rouse no doubts about our mission. In half an hour he left us, giving orders that we should dine with him and his staff in another hour.

Seven round tables were set with six or eight places at each. We sat with the field marshal and his secretary. From the courtyard just outside the window a very fair brass band thundered, "'Nita, Juanita, Ask Thy Soul if We Should Part!'' and other similarly martial airs. Sometimes they broke into a chant in the midst of their playing, Russian fashion, and this was rather stirring. Nothing was said by any of us at the general's table for the first half hour. But our glasses of warm sherry-like wine were filled and refilled rapidly. Each time that Wu drank bottoms-up he showed his empty glass around the circle and we had to do the same. Then at his signal we began to wipe our chopsticks on our sleeves and our breeches and to reach over to the centre of the table for the six or seven different dishes, little lumps of mutton, bean curds, omelet, and dumplings, and so forth.

Our host told us, through his secretary, about Chinese cookery, the soldiers' songs, and the making of wines and spirits, but never a word of politics or the things I wanted most to hear. We ate and drank till the mountainous chief of staff on my right belched in my ear and sweated whole trout brooks from his close-cropped head and the folds in his thick neck. The meal ended, Field Marshal Wu rose, and the band blared a really military tune as Jayne and I found ourselves marching from the room while all the other diners stood at attention. It was difficult not to strut.

Knowing that Wu was very much occupied we refused to sit and talk, but bundled ourselves out and into the staff motor car which was panting by the gateway. The guard was turned out, the band played "Seeing Nellie Home," and we sailed off into the dark singing "Aunt Dinah's Quilting Party." When the car sped to the south gate of Honanfu the narrow way was so blocked by wheelbarrows and vendors of food and cakes and tea that it seemed a teeming bazaar. It was nothing short of murder to charge that crowd. Donkeys and their entire loads took refuge in shops, naked children were snatched up from under our front tires and elderly ladies scaled vertical fences. But as far as I know there was not a single death.

Next morning at six o'clock, by the general's invitation, we set out in rickshaws again for headquarters to meet the escort which was to take us on a day's excursion to the rock chapels of Lungmen, a dozen miles across the river. There were ponies for Jayne and Wang and me, and sixteen cavalrymen of the head-quarters troop to protect us. We scattered the people and drew up before the inn, greatly to the increment of foreign face . . . Four tailors were set feverishly to work on the flags that were to suggest to the bandits that the American Army and Navy were to appear in western China to avenge any insult offered to Jayne or to me.

Langdon Warner, *The Long Old Road in China,* (Doubleday and Company, Inc., copyright 1925, 1926) pp. 5-8.

Portrait of a Warlord

In north China, Feng Yu-hsiang was one of the most powerful and most colorful of the reformist warlords. Feng was a huge man, a compelling speaker with a flair for the dramatic gesture. He was extremely emotional and not infrequently wept publicly. He also affected great simplicity in life and dress; his garb was of the plainest, and he often traveled in a freight car or truck; he denied accumulating money for personal ends, and no evidence exists that he did so.

Feng was the son of a low-ranking army officer, and he spent his childhood in and around army camps. When he was only 16, he joined Li Hung-chang's army, and in 1902 he transferred to Yuan Shih-k'ai's command. Feng advanced steadily in rank, primarily because of his own ability and his extraordinary energy and diligence. With virtually no formal education, he struggled hard to educate himself. He aspired to be first in examinations and com-petitions, and very often gained that distinction. His career was also helped by the fact that he married the niece of one of Yuan Shih-k'ai's trusted subordinates.

Until about 1911 Feng held traditionalistic and conservative views – not unexpected in an ignorant peasant youth. The death of the Manchu Emperor reduced Feng to tears. On the eve of the revolution, however, he came under the influence of some radical officers who persuaded him to help overthrow the monarchy. His superiors put him under arrest, and he was only saved from execution by the influence of his father-in-law, who also managed to get Feng back into Yuan's army shortly after the establishment of the republic.

By the early twentieth century, Westerners had extensive political and economic power over China. At a time of domestic crisis, therefore, the support of Westerners could be helpful. Partly with that in mind, Feng formally adopted the Christian religion in 1914; he had strong puritanical tendencies, and he was impressed by the personal behavior of Christians he observed in China. They did not smoke opium, or drink, or gamble; they educated their children and worked hard, traits Feng admired. He tried to convert his troops to Christianity because he felt they would be more loyal and better disciplined soldiers if they followed Christian moral injunctions. Years later, when Feng was nationally and internationally known, he was called the "Christian General," and many stories circulated about his unique mixture of Christian moralism and Chinese militarism.

It was not only its Christian coloration that made Feng's army unique in China. Feng demanded extraordinary physical fitness, and subjected his officers and men to constant and rigorous training to achieve it. At a time when soldiers were generally expected to be disorderly and officers were assumed to be venal, Feng enforced the most rigid discipline and punished the slightest hint of corruption. He prohibited drinking, gambling, visiting prostitutes, even swearing. Officers were selected on the basis of merit, and were expected to be able to do anything they ordered their men to do. Feng indoctrinated his troops in Christian and Confucian values, stressing both the importance of moral life and the existence of the army as the servant of the people.

Like a number of warlords, Feng controlled many different regions during his career, from a few districts to a province to several provinces. His civil administration demonstrated the same kind of moralistic concerns that his military-training programs did. He vigorously suppressed banditry and disorder, and prohibited vices such as prostitution, gambling, and opium smoking. Feng established several kinds of social-welfare institutions, including rehabilitation centers for beggars, sanatoriums for narcotics addicts, and orphanages. In peacetime, he put his men to work on public projects such as road building, tree planting, and flood control.

Unfortunately, few of Feng's reforms were permanent. The vicissitudes of warlord politics seldom allowed him to remain in one province long enough to carry the programs through, and his successors never concerned themselves with continuing his innovations. Also, Feng seldom had enough money to support his reform proposals adequately; from the outset some were more in the nature of paper changes than substantial realistic innovations. Perhaps the chief weakness of Feng's reform program was his failure to marshal the support and participation of the people he presumably served. Despite the aura of Westernization and innovation given by Feng's Christianity and by the promulgation of reform directives in the context of warlordism, Feng was basically traditional in his thinking. He thought in authoritarian and moralistic terms, not in terms of organizational or institutional change.

Feng participated in many of the warlord wars, and seems to have hoped at one time that he would be able to unify China by force. However, this did not happen, and in 1926 he and his army joined the Kuomintang's Northern Expedition, partly because Feng sympathized with Kuomintang objectives, partly because the prospects of the Northern Expedition looked good, but mainly because the revolutionary army opposed his enemies, Chang Tso-lin and Wu P'ei-fu. When the country was ostensibly united in 1928, Feng was in a powerful position, with high office in the national government and several provinces under his control. Like other warlords, however, he would not accept the leadership of Chiang Kai-shek, and in 1929-30 he joined with Yen Hsi-shan in a bitter, bloody war against Chiang. Chiang won the war and deprived Feng of troop command. His defeat brought his career as a warlord to a close, though he held various sinecures in the national government until his death in 1948.

James E. Sheridan, *China in Disintegration: the Republican Era in Chinese History 1912-1949,* (Macmillan Publishing Company, Inc.) pp. 73-75.

The Chinese Family During the May Fourth Movement

To Chueh-min and Chueh-hui, Chueh-hsin was "Big Brother." Though born of the same mother and living in the same house, his position was entirely different from theirs. In the large Kao family, he was the eldest son of an eldest son, and for that reason his destiny was fixed from the moment he came into the world.

Handsome and intelligent, he was his father's favourite. His private tutor also spoke highly of him. People predicted that he would do big things, and his parents considered themselves fortunate to be blessed with such a son.

Brought up with loving care, after studying with a private tutor for a number of years, Chueh-hsin entered middle school. One of the school's best students, he graduated four years later at the top of his class. He was very interested in physics and chemistry and hoped to go on to a university in Shanghai or Peking, or perhaps study abroad, in Germany. His mind was full of beautiful dreams. At that time he was the envy of his classmates.

In his fourth year at middle school, he lost his mother. His father later married again, this time to a younger woman who had been his mother's cousin. Chueh-hsin was aware of his loss, for he knew full well that nothing could replace the love of a mother. But her death left no irreparable wound in his heart; he was able to console himself with rosy dreams of his future. Moreover, he had someone who understood him and could comfort him – his pretty cousin Mei, "mei" for "plum blossom."

But then, one day, his dreams were shattered, cruelly and bitterly shattered. The evening he returned home carrying his diploma, the plaudits of his teachers and friends still ringing in his ears, his father called him into his room and said:

"Now that you've graduated, I want to arrange your marriage. Your grandfather is looking forward to having a great-grandson, and I, too, would like to be able to hold a grandson in my arms. You're old enough to be married; I won't feel easy until I fulfill my obligation to find you a wife. Although I didn't accumulate much money in my years away from home as an official, still I've put by enough for us to get along on. My health isn't what it used to be; I'm thinking of spending my time at home and having you help me run the household affairs. All the more reason you'll be needing a wife. I've already arranged a match with the Li family. The thirteenth of next month is a good day. We'll announce the engagement then. You can be married within the year. . . ."

The blow was too sudden. Although he understood everything his father said, somehow the meaning didn't fully register. Chueh-hsin only nodded his head. He didn't dare look his father in the eye, although the old man was gazing at him kindly.

Chueh-hsin did not utter a word of protest, nor did such a thought ever occur to him. He merely nodded to indicate his compliance with his father's wishes. But after he returned to his own room, and shut the door, he threw himself down on his bed, covered his head with the quilt and wept. He wept for his broken dreams.

He had heard something about a match with a daughter of the Li family. But he had never been permitted to learn the whole story, and so he didn't place much credence in it. A number of gentlemen with unmarried daughters, impressed by his good looks and his success in his studies, had become interested in him; there was a steady stream of matchmakers to his family's door. His father weeded out the applicants until only two remained under consideration. It was difficult for Mr. Kao to make a choice; both of the persons serving as matchmakers were of equal prestige and importance. Finally, he decided to resort to divination. He wrote each of the girls' names on a slip of red paper, rolled the slips up into balls, then, after praying for guidance before the family ancestral tablets, picked one.

Thus the match with the Li family was decided. But it was only now that Chueh-hsin was informed of the result.

Yes, he had dreamed of romance. The one in his heart was the girl who understood him and who could comfort him – his cousin Mei. At one time he was sure she would be his future mate, and he had congratulated himself that this would be so, since in his family marriage between cousins was quite common.

He was deeply in love with Mei, but now his father had chosen another, a girl he had never seen, and said that he must marry within the year. What's more, his hopes of continuing his studies had burst like a bubble. It was a terrible shock to Chueh-hsin. His future was finished, his beautiful dreams shattered.

He cried his disappointment and bitterness. But the door was closed and Chueh-hsin's head was beneath the bedding. No one knew. He did not fight back, he never thought of resisting. He only bemoaned his fate. But he accepted it. He complied with his father's will without a trace of resentment. But in his heart he wept for himself, ·wept for the girl he adored – Mei, his "plum blossom."

The day of his engagement he was teased and pulled about like a puppet, while at the same time being shown off as treasure of rare worth. He was neither happy nor sad. Whatever people told him to do, he did, as if these acts were duties which he was obliged to perform. In the evening, when the comedy had ended and the guests had departed, Chueh-hsin was exhausted. He went to bed and slept soundly.

After the engagement, he drifted aimlessly from day to day. He stacked his books neatly in the bookcase and didn't look at them again. He played mahjong, went to the opera, drank, and went about making the necessary preparations for his marriage, in accordance with his father's instructions. Chueh-hsin thought very little. He calmly awaited the advent of his bride.

In less than six months, she arrived. To celebrate the marriage, Chueh-hsin's father and grandfather had a stage specially built for the performance of theatricals in the compound.

The marriage ceremony turned out to be not as simple as Chueh-hsin had anticipated. He too, in effect, became an actor, and he had to perform for three days before he was able to obtain his bride. Again he was manipulated like a puppet, again he was displayed as a treasure of rare worth. He was neither happy nor sad – he was only tired, though roused a bit by the general excitement.

This time, however, after his performance was over and the guests departed, he was not able to forget everything and sleep. Because lying in bed beside him was a strange girl. He still had to continue playing a role.

Chueh-hsin was married. His grandfather had obtained a granddaughter-in-law, his father had obtained a daughter-in-law, and others had enjoyed a brief period of merrymaking. The marriage was by no means a total loss for Chueh-hsin either. He had joined in wedlock a tender, sympathetic girl, just as pretty as the one he adored. He was satisfied. For a time he revelled in pleasures he had not believed possible, for a time he forgot his beautiful dreams, forgot the other girl, forgot his lost future. He was sated, he was intoxicated, intoxicated with the tenderness and love of the girl who was his bride. Constantly smiling, he hung about her room all day. People envied him his happiness, and he considered himself very lucky.

Thus one month passed.

One evening his father called him into his room and said:

"Now that you're married you should be earning your own living, or people will talk. I've raised you to manhood and found you a wife. I think we can say that I've fulfilled my duties as a father. From now on you must take care of yourself. We have enough money to send you to a university, down-river, to study, but in the first place you already have a wife; secondly the family property has not yet been shared out among me and my brothers, and I am in charge of the accounts. It would look like favouritism if I advanced money from the family funds for your university education. Besides, your grandfather might not agree. So I've found you a position in the West Szechuan Mercantile Corporation. The salary's not very large, but it will give you and your wife a little spending money. Moreover, if you do your work diligently, you're sure to advance. You start tomorrow. I'll take you down myself. Our family owns some shares in the company and several of the directors are my friends. They'll look after you.''

Chueh-hsin's father spoke in an even voice, as if discussing something quite commonplace. Chueh-hsin listened, and assented. He didn't say whether he was willing or unwilling. There was only one thought in his mind – ''Everything is finished.'' Though he had many words in his heart, he spoke not a one.

The following day after the midday meal his father told him something of how a man going out in the world should behave, and Chueh-hsin made careful mental notes. Sedan-chairs brought him and his father to the door of the West Szechuan Mercantile Corporation. Entering, he first met Manager Huang, a man of about forty with a moustache and a stooped back; Chen, the accountant, who had a face like an old woman; Wang, the tall, emaciated bill-collector; and two or three other ordinary-looking members of the office staff. The manager asked him a few questions; he answered simply, as if by rote. Although they all addressed him very politely, he could tell from their actions and the way they spoke that they were not the same as he. It occurred to him with some surprise that he had seldom met people of this sort before.

His father departed, leaving Chueh-hsin behind. He felt frightened and lonely, a castaway on a desert island. He was not given any work. He just sat in the manager's office and listened to the manager discuss things with various people. After two full hours of this, the manager suddenly noticed him again and said courteously, ''There's nothing for you to do today, Brother. Please come back tomorrow.''

Like a pardoned prisoner, Chueh-hsin happily called a sedan-chair and gave his address. He kept urging the carriers to walk faster. It seemed to him that in all the world there was no place more wonderful than the Kao family compound.

On arriving home, he first reported to his grandfather, who gave him some instructions. Then he went to see·his father, who gave him some more instructions. Finally, he returned to his own apartment. Only here, with his wife questioning him solicitiously and at great length, did he find peace and relaxation.

The next day after breakfast he again went to the corporation and did not return home until five in the afternoon. That day he was given his own office. Under the guidance of the manager and his colleagues, he commenced to work.

Thus, this nineteen-year-old youth took his first big step into the world of business. Gradually, he grew accustomed to his environment and learned a new way of life. Gradually, he forgot all the knowledge he had acquired in his four years of middle school. He began to feel at home in his work. The first time he received his salary of twenty-four *yuan*, he was torn between joy and sorrow. It was the first time he had ever earned any money, yet the pay was also the first fruits of the sale of his career. But as the months went by, the regular installments of twenty-four *yuan* no longer aroused in him any special emotions.

Life was bearable, without happiness, without grief. Although he saw the same faces every day, heard the same uninteresting talk, did the same dull work, all was peaceful and secure. None of the family came to bother him at home; he and his wife were permitted to live quietly.

Less than six months later, another big change occurred in his life. An epidemic struck his father down; all the tears of Chueh-hsin and his brothers and sisters were unable to save him. After his father died, the family burdens were placed on Chueh-hsin's shoulders. In addition to looking after his stepmother, he also became responsible for his two younger sisters and his two young student brothers. Chueh-hsin was then only twenty years of age.

Sorrowfully, he wept for his departed father. He had not thought that fate could be so tragic. But gradually his grief dissipated. After his father was buried, Chueh-hsin virtually forgot him. Not only did he forget his father, he forgot everything that had passed, he forgot his own springtime. Calmly he placed the family burdens on his own young shoulders.

For the first few months they didn't seem very heavy; he was not conscious of any strain. But in a very short time, many arrows, tangible and intangible, began flying in his direction. Some he was able to dodge, but several struck home. He discovered something new, he began to see another side of life in a gentry household. Beneath the surface of peace and affection, hatred and strife were lurking; he also had become a target of attack. Although his surroundings made him forget his springtime, the fires of youth still burned in his heart. He grew angry, he struggled, because he considered himself to be in the right. But his struggles only brought him more troubles and more enemies.

The Kao family was divided into four households. Originally Chueh-hsin's grandfather had five sons, but the second son had died many years ago. Uncle Ke-ming and his Third Household were on fairly good terms with the First Household, which Chueh-hsin now headed. But the Fourth and Fifth Households were very unfriendly to Chueh-hsin; the wives of both secretly waged a relentless battle against him and his First Household, and spread countless rumours about him.

Struggling didn't do the least bit of good, and he was exhausted. What's the use of this endless strife? he wondered. Those women would never change and he couldn't make them give in. Why waste energy looking for trouble? Chueh-hsin evolved a new way of managing affairs – or perhaps it would be better to say of managing the family. He ended his battle with the women. He pretended to go along with their wishes whenever he could. Treating them with deference, he joined them in mahjong, he helped them with their shopping. . . . In brief, he sacrificed a portion of his time to win his way into their good graces. All he wanted was peace and quiet.

Not long after, the elder of his two young sisters died of tuberculosis. Although he mourned for her, his heart felt somewhat eased, for her death lightened his burden considerably.

Some time later, his first child was born – a boy. Chueh-hsin felt an immense gratitude towards his wife. The coming of this son into the world brought him great happiness. He himself was a man without hope; he would never have the chance to fulfill his beautiful dreams. His only function in life was to bear a load on his shoulders, to maintain the family his father had left behind. But now he had a son, his own flesh and blood. He would raise the child lovingly, and see in him the realization of the career he had lost. The boy was part of him and the boy's happiness would be his own. Chueh-hsin found consolation in this thought. He felt that his sacrifices were not in vain.

Two years later, in 1919, the May Fourth Movement began. Fiery, bitter newspaper articles awakened in Chueh-hsin memories of his youth. Like his two younger brothers, he avidly read the Peking dispatches carried in the local press, and news of the big strike in Shanghai on June third which followed. When the local paper reprinted articles from the *New Youth* and *Weekly Review* magazines, he hurried to the only bookstore in town that was selling these journals, and bought the latest issue of the first, and two or three issues of the second. Their words were like sparks, setting off a conflagration in the brothers' hearts. Aroused by the fresh approach and the ardent phrases, the brothers found themselves in complete agreement with the writers' sentiments.

Therefore they bought up all the progressive periodicals they could lay their hands on, including back numbers. Every night he and his two brothers would take turns reading every one of these, without skipping even the letters to the editor. Sometimes they had lively discussions on subjects raised in the periodicals. Chueh-hsin's brothers were more radical than he was, for he was only a follower of Hu Shih, whose "On Ibsenism" even seemed a little too extreme to him. He was an admirer of Liu Pan-nung's "philosophy of compliant bows," and he liked Tolstoy's "principle of non-resistance."

Indeed, Chueh-hsin found the "compliant bow" philosophy and the "policy of non-resistance" most useful. It was thanks to them that he was able to reconcile, with no difficulty at all, the theories expressed in *New Youth* with the realities of his big family. They were a solace to him, permitting him to believe in the new theories while still conforming to the old feudal concepts. He saw no inconsistency.

Chueh-hsin became a man with a split personality. In the old society, in the midst of his old-fashioned family, he was a spineless, supine Young Master; in the company of his brothers, he was a youth of the new order.

Naturally, this way of life was something the younger boys could not understand. They berated Chueh-hsin for it frequently, and he placidly accepted their criticism. But he continued to read new books and periodicals, and continued to live in the same old-fashioned manner.

He watched his first son learning to crawl, then to walk, then to speak a few simple words. The child was adorable, intelligent, and Chueh-hsin lavished nearly all his affection on him. "He's going to do all the things I couldn't," thought Chueh-hsin. He refused to hire a wet-nurse, insisting that his wife suckle the child herself. Fortunately, she had enough milk. Such goings-on were virtually unprecedented in a wealthy family, and they led to a great deal of gossip. But Chueh-hsin bore it all, convinced that he was acting in the child's best interests.

Every night, after his wife and child had retired, he would sit beside them, feasting his eyes on the baby sleeping in its mother's arms. Looking at the child's face, he was able to forget about himself completely. Chueh-hsin couldn't resist planting a kiss on the baby's satiny cheek. He softly breathed words of thanks and hope and love, rather vague words, but they gushed naturally from his lips like water from a fountain.

Chueh-hsin didn't know that his parents had loved him with the same fervour when he was an infant. They too had breathed words of thanks and hope and love.

Pa Chin, *Family,* (Doubleday and Company, Inc.) 1972, pp. 35-44.

7

The Kuo Min Tang

Sung Chiao-jen's assassination and Sun Yat-sen's decision to go underground and then to ally with the Comintern ended the promise of the Kuo Min Tang as an open, western, democratic political party. But it was far from dead. After its alliance with the Comintern and the Chinese Communist party in 1923, it grew militarily as well as politically more active. Capitalizing on the understandable desire to reunify the country after a time of disorder, as well as the distaste and hatred of most Chinese for the foreigners who had become the symbol of oppression to them, the Kuo Min Tang began putting together an apparatus for conquest and a return to centralized rule. Although the idea of a dynasty was dead in China, many believed an appropriate substitute to be a strong political party buttressed by military strength and headed by an unquestioned, impressive and absolute leader.

This leader was Sun Yat-sen, but he died of cancer in 1925. Who would inherit his mantle? As Sun Yat-sen's chief military assistant, Chiang K'ai-shek had been sent to Moscow for training soon after the agreement with the Comintern in 1923. He was a nationalist and a Confucian, and he grew very suspicious of the universal and materialistic nature of communism. Although he learned much in the field of military tactics, he became worried that the Russians' interest and influence in China would in the long run also prove imperialistic.

When he returned to China in 1924, Chiang was made head of the new Whampoa Academy, which had been set up near Canton with five hundred students being trained to lead the military crusade which Sun planned to accompany his political takeover. Never again was Sun going to be left with enthusiasm and ideas but no power! In the spirit of the 1923 alliance, Chiang worked closely with Communists, including Chou En-lai, a young intellectual who had been converted to communism when he was in France during the first World War. Chou and Chiang each tried to outfox the other. Chiang held on tightly to the Russian arms which had been given to them and maneuvered to keep Communists out of the most powerful positions. Chou constantly tried to gain adherents among the more left-leaning of the Kuo Min Tang regulars, and to innitrate where it was not possible to persuade.

A series of labor strikes which were essentially nationalistic (mostly anti-British) gave the KMT its opportunity for a military offensive. The strikes started in Shanghai in 1925. Although organized largely by members of the Chinese Communist Party, they focused on the evils of imperialism rather than those of capitalism. British over-reaction to these demonstrations inflamed anti-foreign sentiment even further, led to more protests, boycotts, and finally violence in both Shanghai and Canton, where Whampoa cadets were involved and fifty-two Chinese were killed by French and British troops who were protecting their property.

Arguing that only a strong and united (if admittedly undemocratic) China could ever repel the foreigners and start the process of modernization on China's own terms, the Kuo Min Tang, with their Communist allies, started marching northward from Canton in the summer of 1926. The march northward was accomplished easily, thanks to advanced propaganda work, agreements with local warlords, and the people's readiness for a return to centralism.

Facing little opposition, the KMT nevertheless struggled with internal problems: how best to keep their soldiers in order when marching through the countryside, what to do about the Communists, whose loyalty to the Nationalist Revolution was temporary at best, and how fast to throw off the help of the westerners whom they hoped to replace?

Once in Central China, these tensions prompted a split between the right wing forces, mostly military, and the left wing. Chiang, heading the right wing, moved to take over the rich industrial area of the lower Yangtze, including Shanghai and Nanking. The left wing of the Kuo Min Tang, with at least three Communists in top posts, was centered in Wuhan further west on the Yangtze. In April, 1927 evidence was found in the Soviet Embassy in Peking that the Russians were attempting subversion in various ways, including alliances with both the Communists and the Nationalists. This was the ammunition Chiang needed to launch a campaign against the Communists who had so recently been his comrades, and he lost no time in acting on the evidence. He suppressed the labor movement, executed Communist leaders, and managed to demoralize and intimidate the whole left wing of the party. This was the famous Nanking-Wuhan split.

Chiang had much to do besides the exasperating job of controlling the leftists and Communists. In 1928 he completed the ostensible unification of China by occupying Peking ("Northern Capital"), renaming it Peiping ("Northern Peace") because he wanted to keep the nation's capital in Nanking, where his base was by now firmly established. Chiang's air of authority, his endorsement of Christianity, his anti-communism and obvious desire to modernize won him friends among the westerners. They were now prepared to promise that if he would establish a reliable banking system, varied industrial base, and modern government, they would be willing to renegotiate the "unequal treaties," withdraw their claims to extraterritoriality, and return tariff supervision to the Chinese government.

During the late twenties and early thirties there was much evidence of sincerity on both sides. The Chinese government achieved important reforms in the areas of civil and criminal law, tariff collection, salt revenue and the post office. Many hospitals and schools were built during this time, usually with foreign capital. Far from exploiting the Chinese, the westerners were of undoubted benefit to them, but their influence was confined mainly to the cities. The number of foreign "concessions" was sharply reduced, from 33 to 13, and within each concession was a greater (although grudging) realization that "rights recovery," Chiang's chief aim in foreign policy, was entirely within normal Chinese expectations, and that nineteenth century imperialism would have to be abandoned in China as well as in other places.

Chiang's hurdles in trying to modernize China were tremendous, but there was much energy in the Kuo Min Tang during the late twenties and early thirties. Substantial accomplishments were made during this period, later to be wiped out by subsequent developments. The railroad system was extremely sketchy, requiring a large outlay of capital for a deferred reward. Such capital might well have to come from the West, involving the proud young Chinese nationalists still further in western indebtedness. The situation for industrial development was similar. Although the Chinese built up cotton, cigarette and cement manufacturing, for example, they were not able to develop heavy industry or sophisticated machinery which would have made them truly independent of western technology.

Chiang succeeded in setting up two banking systems with the help of his wily brother-in-law, T.V. Soong. One system dealt with the West, the other with the interior of China. Each was a vast improvement over China's old high-interest private lenders. Although for both banking and fiscal policy the government was forced to rely on financiers whose own fortunes were substantial and growing more so, many necessary first steps were taken during these early days.

During normal times the Nanking government might have carried off a slow, sure modernization, a recovery of China's dignity among the other large nations without the need for war, perhaps even a slow democratization and an extension of the benefits of industrialization to the poor peasantry. But there were three elements militating against this. First, Chiang's power base was filled with "strange bedfellows," groups which shifted and which

Chiang K'ai-shek and his Wife, Soong Mei-ling

under most circumstances couldn't be expected to get along with each other. Virtually none had direct knowledge of the needs of the peasant. Many were western-educated although their main hold on the affections of the Chinese people was that they had promised to get rid of the westerners in China. Chiang's own wife, one of the famous Soong sisters, had been educated at Wellesley College near Boston, Massachusetts and she opened up many new western and western-educated contacts to him. Rumor has it that Chiang was so eager for a connection with this rich and powerful family that he proposed first to Mei-ling's older sister, the widow of Sun Yat-sen, and, when refused, settled on her younger sister, divorcing his wife and agreeing to adopt Christianity in order to do so. Besides the West/anti-West tensions, Chiang had followers among the military and the anti-military, the democratic and the anti-democratic, those who would extend power and wealth to the countryside, and those who feared the peasants. It was a difficult balancing act, one which was forced on Chiang by circumstances, but also one for which his personality seemed suited.

The second factor which prevented Chiang's success in China was his increasing absorption with his own juggling act rather than with China's deepening crisis. His was a superficial approach, seizing the problems which seemed most pressing and closest, searching for the simplest solutions, many of which were foolish and terroristic. When the Communists have been driven out of a province, send in the Y.M.C.A.! If you need more money, print it! If someone is bothering you, eliminate him! His relationships with the Japanese, the Communists, even the westerners were marked by shifting policies and erratic behavior. But to everyone he seemed an extraordinary person. In him always was the intensity, the spare, self-contained appearance in the midst of power and luxury, which made people follow him even when they could not be sure what he would do next, or to whom:

> He attracted loyalty and respect not through political inspiration as Sun Yat-sen did, but by the magnetism of an impressive personality. He was slim, laconic and expressionless except for alert dark eyes which seemed to pierce through as if from an inner head behind a mask. His great talent was not military but political, exercised through a mastery of balance among factions and plots so that he came to be called the "Billiken" after the weighted doll that cannot be knocked over.*

The third factor which interrupted China's attempt at government and modernization under the Kuo Min Tang was the war with Japan. The Washington Conference of 1922 placed much more confidence in its participants than they deserved. To balance Japan's smaller ship ratio, the United States promised not to arm its Pacific colonies. This made it possible for the Pacific to be turned into what one participant described as a "Japanese lake." In 1931 the Japanese tested the waters when some young officers forced a confrontation with Chinese soldiers. The succeeding takeover was called the "Mukden Incident," and, once committed, the Japanese quickly took over Manchuria. Although this is

*Barbara W. Tuchman, *Stilwell and the American Experience in China 1911-1945,* (New York, 1972), p. 117.

an area north of the wall, and although the Manchus were never considered to be full-fledged Chinese, still Manchuria had for centuries been considered part of China. Thus it was a tremendous shock to many when the Japanese easily defeated the Chinese warlord, Chang Hsueh-liang, an ally of Chiang K'ai-shek's, and forced him southward into northern China.

In spite of the boldness of the Japanese move, the Chinese reaction was minimal and ineffective. Chiang sent no reinforcement to Chang. Chinese merchants and consumers staged a boycott of Japanese goods which was quite successful but unofficial. The League of Nations was impotent. The United States contented itself with a rather weak reaction, "non-recognition," to Japan's take-over of Manchuria. The European powers, as the thirties progressed, were more and more absorbed with the Hitler menace.

After a short period of bombing Shanghai in 1932, where they met firm resistance from Chiang's troops, the Japanese concentrated on extending their power over Manchuria. Between 1932 and 1937 the Japanese also moved into Mongolia, and then into northern China, as traders of many goods, including opium, and as propagandists for an Asian trading arrangement which would replace Chiang's dependence on the westerners. The Japanese also capitalized on the relatively weak hold of the KMT on the north, and on the resentment felt by many northern Chinese when the capital had been moved to Nanking. Thus the uneasy truce simmered in the mid-1930's.

Meanwhile Chiang built up his military forces, accepting help from German advisors, and concentrating on training and equipment instead of the mass mobilization which many patriots advocated. Accused of not fighting Japan effectively enough while he still kept harassing the Communists, Chiang replied that while the Japanese were a disease of the skin, the Communists were a disease of the heart. But by July 1937 there was another "incident," this on the Marco Polo Bridge in Peking, in which, again, Japanese and Chinese soldiers suddenly found themselves fighting. After that, but still calling the hostilities an "incident," as opposed to a war, the Japanese poured into eastern China. They took most cities easily, but Nanking was more difficult. As the capital, this city had been a center for anti-Japanese feeling, and once it was taken, the Japanese soldiers were set loose to perform whatever acts of atrocity and revenge they wanted. The "rape of Nanking," especially hard on civilians, old and young, aroused the sympathy of the world. Europe, though, was more than ever concerned with its own problems, and the United States was still paralyzed in its determination to stay neutral.

Chiang was finally forced to resist the Japanese. His kidnapping in Sian in December 1937 by frantic officers in Chang Hsueh-liang's army who were eager to attack the Japanese instead of their fellow Chinese, had convinced Chiang to join the Communists in a "United Front" which would aim at getting Japan out of China. But at first the Japanese troops were so overwhelming that Chiang decided to "trade space for time," to pull his government further to the west in China. All along the Yangtze River, for as far as one could see, those who could move were carrying their possessions, or their office material, or their children toward the west.

By 1940 Japan had occupied much of eastern China, at least its cities and its railroad lines, and Chiang had been forced to withdraw his government to Chungking, in Szechwan, past the steep Yangtze gorges in the west of China. Although savagely bombed, this position was safe from the Japanese armies, but it was also isolated not only from his European and American allies but from the vast majority of Chiang's Chinese supporters in the more industrialized part of China. Ever the chameleon, Chiang soon shed the liberalism of his Shanghai banker surroundings of earlier days and took on the conservatism of the Szechwan land-owners who were now his chief supporters. He grew even more frightened of land reform than he had been before. In spite of its alliances with the CCP, the KMT now turned against the idea of mass mobilization or arming of peasants, gave its "People's Political Council" only advisory powers, and assigned more and more of the civil government's powers to the military. This tightening of government control often happens in wartime, even in democracies, but Chiang was now in complete control of the government (see document #3) and his armies were still strangely quiet.

In place of earnest and consistent attempts to tackle the poverty and distress which more than ever overwhelmed the people, Chiang proposed moral awakening. In the "New Life Movement" during the 1930's, he had criticized the people for not being military-minded enough. At the same time he proposed a "new spiritualism," very like Confucianism, which would help the Chinese peasant withstand his personal poverty and despair by concentrating on the problems of his country. Criticizing the "urge to acquire material gain" in the same way that Confucius had criticized "profit," he urged his fellow Chinese to return in-stead to the spiritual ideas which distinguished them as Chinese: " 'Li,' courtesy; 'I,' service toward one's fellow men and toward oneself; 'Lien,' honesty and respect for the rights of others; and

'Chih,' high-mindedness and honor.''* Despite propaganda work in the countryside, these slogans never really caught on. Then in 1943, in *China's Destiny,* Chiang attempted to pin all of China's troubles on the foreign powers which, he claimed, had humiliated her for decades. True though this seemed at the time, this was not the whole story, and made Chiang seem defensive and self-serving.

Cut off from old tax bases and unable to develop new ones, Chiang simply issued notes to pay his bills. He and his followers swelled the population and exhausted the resources of Chungking, and the combination of unbased paper money, corruption and overcrowding led to inflation. United States aid to Chungking was enormous, but was concentrated mostly on military equipment, which was the immediate problem, rather than on stabilizing the economy or offering long-standing support. Chiang, in any case, preferred firearms to advice, and in the wartime atmosphere it was heresy to doubt that he and only he "spoke for" the "Chinese people."

At the end of the war in 1945, China had seen its government absorbed in purely military concerns for eight years, cooped up as imperious visitors in a rural, mountainous and alien part of China, demoralized and without any ideas except those centering on its own survival. In this atmosphere old animosities hardened, thinking became narrower and more rigid, and corruption flourished. Chiang's own asceticism and rectitude remained, but he seemed inflexible and blind to the corruption which abounded among his associates.

When the Chinese government was airlifted by the Americans back into the eastern cities after the war (to make sure it was the Nationalists, and not the Communists, who got there first), they took many of Chungking's problems with them. The inflation worsened monthly, and was probably the greatest the world has ever seen. Government workers used to have to push their week's pay home in wheelbarrows, only then to spend it even more quickly. Finally the middle class, which had always supported the Kuo Min Tang, began to suffer, and to wonder whether anyone was in charge.

Disillusion is to be expected after an experience as exhausting and tragic as the war and the inflation. Most humans cannot resist the urge to pin that disillusion, which is such an uncomfortable emotion, on someone else. Chiang's isolation, his lack of emotion,

*From an article by Madame Chiang quoted by Franz Schurmann and Orville Schell, *Republican China,* (New York, 1967), p. 152.

even his beautiful and imperial-looking wife, all became liabilities to him. The Chinese might have forgiven him for his ineffectiveness – at least for a while. But once he was no longer perceived of as a good man, a sensitive leader aware of their suffering, he had lost his hold on the loyalty of the people, and so he lost as well the "mandate" which was still subtly at work in Chinese politics.

Description of Chiang Kai-shek

For all that any observer might see, the years of war dealt kindly with Chiang Kai-shek. His face changed by scarcely a line or a wrinkle. Always immaculate, always encased in an armor of self-discipline, he preserved his personality safe from the prying curiosity of the public. Countless mass meetings hung upon the short-clipped words he shrilled forth in his high-pitched Chekiang accent. None ever saw him kindled by the emotion that flickered from the adoring crowds; none ever saw him acknowledge the surging cheers with more than a slow, taut smile or the quick bob-bing of his head.

Only the most convulsive moment of emotion can make him lift the hard casing of control in public and show the man beneath. In August 1945 Chiang sat quietly in a stuffy radio station in Chungking waiting to tell the Chinese people that the war was over. He was, as always, fixedly composed. His pate was shaven clean, and no telltale fuzz indicated graying hair. His spotless khaki tunic, barren of any decoration, was tightly buttoned at the throat and buckled with a Sam Browne belt; a fountain pen was clipped in his pocket. The studio was hot, and the twenty people in the room oozed sweat; only the Generalissimo seemed cool. He ad-justed hornrimmed glasses, glanced at the scarlet flowers on the table before him, and slowly turned to the microphone to inform the people in his clear, high voice that victory had been won. As he spoke, a loudspeaker outside the building spread the news; and crowds, recognizing his conspicuous sedan, began to gather out-side the stone building. He could hear the faint sound of cheers.

Chiang finished in ten minutes. Then suddenly his head sagged; beneath his dark eyes the pouches of sleeplessness let go; the muscles of his slight body relaxed in profound exhaustion. For a fleeting moment the smooth exterior was punctured, the weariness and strain breaking through at the moment of victory to show the man. As quickly as the mood came it was gone, and he walked out of the studio, passed through the crowd with a smiling nod here and there, then sped back to his home. Watching him descend the stairs through the crowd to his sedan, no one could tell that here was a man who had just seen the defeat of his national enemy and who, only that night, was about to set in motion the wheels of machinery that was to engulf the country afresh in civil war.

Chiang's personal discipline is one of the first clues to his complex, involved character. It has been bred of a tempestuous, storm-tossed life and, like his lust for power, his calculating ruthlessness, his monumental stubbornness, has become more than an individual characteristic – it is a force in national politics. Chiang's character reflects and distorts fifty of the most turbulent years in Chinese history.

Chiang Kai-shek was born (in 1888) into the home of a small Chekiang farmer, a member of the governing group of the village, at a moment when China was entering a period of almost unprecedented chaos and disaster. His boyhood was sad. On his fifteenth birthday he wrote:

> "My father died when I was nine years old. . . . The miserable condition of my family at that time is beyond description. My family, solitary and without influence, became at once the target of much insult and maltreatment. . . . It was entirely due to my mother and her kindness and perseverance that the family was saved from utter ruin. For a period of seventeen years – from the age of nine until I was twenty-five years old – my mother never spent a day free from domestic difficulties."

China, in Chiang's boyhood, was prey to every humiliation foreign arms could heap on her, and Chiang, moved by the national disaster, chose to become a soldier. He studied briefly in Japan, then returned to participate in the competitive examinations for admission to the first Chinese military academy, at Paoting. He passed these examinations with distinction and within a year had marked himself as one of the academy's outstanding students. He was one of a handful chosen by the academy in 1907 to be trained in Japan, and there he was soon selected to serve with a Japanese field artillery regiment as a cadet. He did not like Japan and later spoke bitterly of his service there. But he did like military life. Once he told a group of Chinese students who had joined his army none too voluntarily:

> "When I was a young man, I made up my mind to become a soldier. I have always believed that to be in the army is the highest experience of human existence as well as the highest form of revolutionary activity. All that I now possess in experience, knowledge, spirit, and personality I gained through military training and experience."

While he was in Japan, he was stirred, like other student thinkers, by Sun Yat-sen's vision of a new China, strong and great. In 1911 he returned to China to join the uprising that overthrew the Manchus and established the Chinese Republic. When the first republic proved a mockery, he went to Shanghai; what he did there is a matter of gossip and guess, for official biographies skip hastily over this period. It is known, though, that he was helped by a revolutionary named Ch'en Chi-mei, uncle of the CC brothers. In 1915 Chiang participated in another military coup aimed at seizing the Kiangnan arsenal near Shanghai. His comrades of that adventure, who are still among his intimate associates, fled the country, but Chiang disappeared somewhere into Shanghai's murky underworld. He lived a fast, hard life of personal danger, hunger, and abandon; then for a while he was an inconspicuous clerk on the Shanghai stock exchange. At that time, the underworld of Shanghai was dominated by the notorious Green Gang that controlled the city's rackets of opium, prostitution, and extortion. The Green Gang was an urban outgrowth of one of the many secret societies that have flourished in China for centuries. Such a gang has no counterpart in Western life; it sank its roots into all the filth and misery of the great lawless city, disposed of its gunmen as it saw fit, protected its clients by violence, was an organized force perhaps more powerful than the police. The border line between violent insurrectionary and outright gangster was often blurred; men passed between the two worlds with ease. No biographer can trace Chiang's precise degree of association with the Green Gang; but no informed Chinese denies the association, and no account of China's Revolution fails to record that at every crisis in Shanghai, the gang acted in his support.

Out from the mists of Shanghai, Chiang Kai-shek strode forth into the full blaze of Chinese national politics at Canton in the summer of 1924. Precisely how he arrived at this eminence from his previous estate of penniless dependency on the Shanghai publicans is obscure. He served briefly with a Fukienese warlord after Shanghai; he had been brought to Sun Yat-sen's attention by his Shanghai friends, and Sun sent him to study Russian military techniques at Moscow in 1923. He had returned to China and Canton with a huge distrust of the Russians but a shrewd appreciation of the methods of the one-party state. Canton in those days was bursting with fresh energy and new ideas. Kuomintang leaders argued and competed; intrigue dissolved and remade political alliances. During the two years of Chiang's stay in Canton he was never beaten in a quarrel. He staged his first successful armed coup in the spring of 1926 against the left wing of his own party; it was a masterful piece of timing, and after Sun Yat-sen's death he succeeded to the post of party leader.

During the next twenty years both China and Chiang changed, but his dominance in the Kuomintang was never once seriously threatened. His one passion now became and remained an overriding lust for power. All his politics revolved about the concept of force. He had grown up in a time of treachery and violence. There were few standards of human decency his early warlord contemporaries did not violate; they obeyed no law but power, and Chiang outwitted them at their own game. His false starts in insurrection had taught him that he should show no mercy to the vanquished and that the victor remains victor only as long as his armies are intact. When he started north from Canton in 1926 to seize the Yangtze Valley, he was an accomplished student in all the arts of buying men or killing them.

A full decade elapsed between the success of the Nationalist Revolution in 1927 and the invasion by the Japanese in 1937, a decade in which the frail, brooding figure of Chiang Kai-shek grew ever larger and more meaningful in the life of China. Chiang was shrewd – only a shrewd man could have built up his power from that of an insurrectionary to that of a leader willing and able to offer combat to the Japanese Empire. He knew how to draw on the Shanghai business world for support in money and goods; he was student enough to bring some of China's finest scholars into his administration. Power had come to Chiang Kai-shek as he rode the crest of a revolution to triumph over the warlords; the wave receded, but Chiang consolidated his victory on a new basis. He still spoke of a Nationalist Revolution – but the fact that the Revolution involved the will of the people escaped him. Chiang relied not on the emotion of the peasant masses but on an army and its guns.

Theodore H. White and Annalee Jacoby, *Thunder Out of China,* (William Morrow and Co., copyright 1946 by William Sloane Associates, Inc.; renewed 1974 by Theodore H. White and Annalee Jacoby), pp. 118-121.

Excerpts from Chiang K'ai-shek's Writings

Why Is a New Life Needed?

The general psychology of our people today can be described as spiritless. What manifests itself in behavior is this: lack of discrimination between good and evil, between what is public and what is private, and between what is primary and what is secondary. Because there is no discrimination between good and evil, right and wrong are confused; because there is no discrimination between public and private, improper taking and giving (of public funds) occur; and because there is no distinction between primary and secondary, first and last are not placed in the proper order. As a result, officials tend to be dishonest and avaricious, the masses are undisciplined and calloused, the youth become degraded and intemperate, the adults are corrupt and ignorant, the rich become extravagant and luxurious, and the poor become mean and disorderly. Naturally it has resulted in disorganization of the social order and national life, and we are in no position either to prevent or to remedy national calamities, disasters caused from within, or invasions from without. The individual, society and the whole country are now suffering. If the situation should remain unchanged, it would become impossible even to continue living under such miserable conditions. In order to develop the life of our nation, protect the existence of our society, and improve the livelihood of our people, it is absolutely necessary to wipe out these unwholesome conditions and to start to lead a new and rational life.

By observing these virtues (decorum, righteousness, integrity, and a sense of shame), it is hoped that social disorder and individual weakness will be remedied and the people will become more military-minded. If a country cannot defend itself, it has every chance of losing its existence . . . Therefore our people must have military training. As a preliminary, we must acquire the habits of orderliness, cleanliness, simplicity, frugality, promptness, and exactness. We must preserve order, emphasize organization, responsibility, and discipline, and be ready to die for the country at any moment.

In conclusion, the life of our people will be elevated if we live artistically; we will become wealthy if we live productively; and we will be safe if we lead a military way of life. When we do this, we will have a rational life. This rational life is founded on li, i, lien, and ch'ih. The four virtues, in turn, can be applied to food, clothing, shelter and action. If we can achieve this, we will have revolutionized the daily life of our people and laid the foundation for the rehabilitation of our nation.

From *China's Destiny*:

During the last hundred years, under the oppression of the unequal treaties, the life of the Chinese people became more and more degenerate. Everyone took self-interest as the standard of right and wrong, and personal desires as the criterion of good and evil; a thing was considered as right if it conformed to one's self-interest or good if it conformed to one's personal desires . . .

China's ancient ethical teachings and philosophies contained detailed and carefully worked out principles and rules for the regulation and maintenance of the social life of man. The structure of our society underwent many changes, but our social life never deviated from the principles governing the relationship between father and son, husband and wife, brother and brother, friend and friend, superior and inferior, man and woman, old and young, as well as principles enjoining mutual help among neighbors and care of the sick and weak . . .

Individuals, striving singly, will not achieve great results, nor lasting accomplishments. Consequently, all adult citizens and promising youths whether in a town, a district, a province, or in the country at large, should have a common organization with a systematic plan for binding the members together and headquarters to promote joint reconstruction activities and also personal accomplishments. Only by working with such a central organization can individuals live up to Dr. Sun Yat-sen's words: "To dedicate the few score years of our perishable life to the laying of an imperishable foundation for our nation." . . .

That unity does not last is due to hypocrisy and the best antidote for hypocrisy is sincerity. Incapacity to unite is the result of selfishness, and the best antidote for selfishness is public spirit. . . .

Members of the San Min Chu I Youth Corps will receive strict training and observe strict discipline. They will promote all phases of the life of the people, and protect the interests of the entire nation. It will be their mission to save the country from decline and disorganization, to wipe out national humiliation, to restore national strength, and to show loyalty to the state and filial devotion to the nation. They should emulate the sages and heroes of history and be the life blood of the people and the backbone of the nation. They should understand that the orders issued by the Corps are aimed at sustaining the collective life of the youth of the whole nation, and that the strong organization of the Corps will help them to achieve their common objective, namely, the success of our National Revolution in the realization of the Three Principles of the People. . . .

Considering the state as an organism as far as life is concerned, we may say that the Three Principles constitute the soul of our nation, because without these Principles our national reconstruction would be deprived of its pivot. If all the·revolutionary elements and promising youths in the country really want to throw in their lot with the fate of the country, if they regard national undertakings as their own undertakings and the national life as their own life – then, they should all enlist in the Kuomintang or in the Youth Corps. By so doing, they can discharge the highest duties of citizenship and attain the highest ideal in life. Then and only then can our great mission of national reconstruction be completed.

Excerpts are from Wm. Theodore de Bary, ed., *Sources of Chinese Tradition,* (Columbia University Press, 1960), pp. 801-812.

A partial listing of Chiang K'ai-shek's positions in the Chinese government during the war against Japan:

Chief Executive of the Kuomintang

President of the National Government

Chairman of the National Military Council

Commander-in-Chief of land, naval, and air forces

Supreme Commander, China Theatre

President of the State Council

Chairman of the Supreme National Defense Council

Director-General of the Central Planning Board

Chairman of the Party and Political Work Evaluation Committee

Director of the New Life Movement Association

Chairman of the Commission for Inauguration of Constitutional Government

President of the Central Training Corps

President of the School for Descendants of Revolutionary Martyrs

President of the National Glider Association

8

The Communist Party
Before "Liberation"

To trace the history of the Communist Party in China one must backtrack from the times of the Kuo Min Tang and the Second World War, and go all the way back to the May Fourth Movement. Strange though it may seem, it was the May Fourth Movement, with its emphasis on the liberation of the human mind from crippling tradition, and on the enormous variety of choices possible in life, which produced the infant Communist Party. A one-party system, with only one dogma and one approach, came to seem attractive after years of trying other philosophies and finding them weak and confusing. As one early Communist put it:

> I am now able to impose order on all the ideas which I could not reconcile; I have found the key to all the problems which seemed to me self-contradictory and insoluble.*

The Party was actually founded in 1921 by Ch'en Tu-hsiu, the wealthy young man who had been the editor of the influential *New Youth* magazine. He had been inspired both by his years in France, where he found the principles of the French Revolution particularly exciting, and by the example of the Bolshevik takeover in Russia. At closer hand to inspire him was his friend Gregory Voitinsky, a Comintern agent. A very small group at first, they were lent prestige by their work in the labor movement and their backing by the Comintern. Their biggest problem was to decide whom they were representing: was it the working class only, or should they also work with poor peasants and even, in a "United Front," with the bourgeoisie and the KMT?

Comintern instructions tended to encourage contacts with the wider spectrum, emphasizing the gradual approach as the least foolhardy. They also insisted that the Communists could put the energy of the nationalist movement to their own advantage by, as they put it, riding on its back. The "United Front" policy,

*Quoted in Fairbank, Reischauer and Craig, *East Asia: The Modern Transformation,* (Boston, 1965), p. 672.

however, was fraught with danger for the Communists. How could one stay truly close to one's beliefs and truly revolutionary if one was willing to work with nearly anyone? In 1927 after the Nanking-Wuhan split, the Comintern changed its approach, rejected its past "opportunism" and condemned Ch'en Tu-hsiu and his colleagues for vacillating too much and for being willing to entertain what were now termed as "unrevolutionary theories." More secrecy and more armed uprisings were now urged. Since many of the "United Front" theories had been considered originally at the behest of the Comintern itself, confidence in Moscow began to weaken. But the "new line" didn't have much success either. This more active, frankly-left approach led to the "Autumn Harvest Rising" in 1927 in Hunan, in central China, the home base of Huang Hsing and other revolutionary heroes. It has long been said of Hunan province that the red peppers which grow there, often hanging from the eaves of the houses, are what make Hunanese so strong and volatile. Hunan, it is said, has produced some of China's best scholars and best generals. Success in those fields often depends on the willingness to look at things from an entirely new perspective. Can it be that the Hunanese do this well because they had their brains expanded by eating hot peppers when they were two years old?

The "Autumn Harvest Rising" was undertaken on Party orders by a young and unknown Hunanese Party worker named Mao Tse-tung. But this and other attempted takeovers of isolated posts in the countryside were short-lived, and they and what was now called the "Putschist line" were all discredited. The Party grew weaker and weaker.

During the late twenties the Party staggered under the twin blows of Chiang's hostility and its own uncertainty as to the best way to proceed. As good Marxists they knew that they should believe that their only true allies were the industrial workers in the cities. There were very few of them, however, and furthermore, even they were not flocking to the Communist Party. In fact, their percentage in the Party was steadily decreasing. Finally, after a disastrous attempt to capture Changsha in Hunan in 1930, the leaders of the Chinese Communist Party were criticized, along with the notion that all "Truth" came from Moscow.

Although the Party's Central Committee remained in Shanghai, the real idea center of the Party moved after the Changsha disaster to the Ching Kang Shan mountains on the Hunan-Kiangsi border. Since each province's control tended to be weakest at its edges, it was a good place for them to set up their base unmolested by the

IMPORTANT AREAS
IN CHINESE COMMUNIST HISTORY

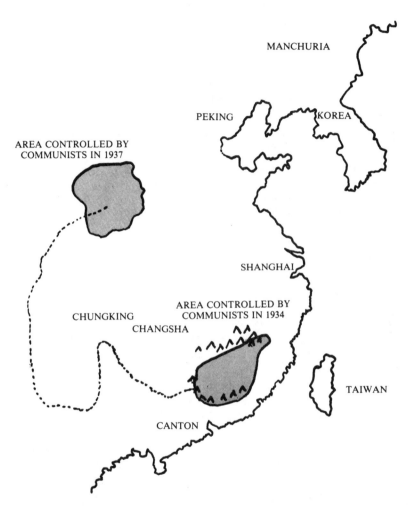

authorities. Instead of concentrating on short-lived control over a
city, they attempted the solid and more permanent domination of
a section of the countryside. And instead of relying on the city
workers, they pitched their appeal to the bitter and impoverished
peasants. They built up the food supplies and began to develop
policies, centering mainly around land reform, designed to win
them new supporters among the large population of tenant
farmers. Using the "border region" idea, they built on their

reputation as underdogs, and gathering about 10,000 men, they proceeded to build the Red Army.

The Red Army was fashioned around a strategy which was very old in China. It had been described in the Sun-tzu, a Chou dynasty treatise on the art of war, but was forgotten until it was revived by Mao and his military colleague, Chu Teh. Sun-tzu's methods emphasized movement, flexibility and surprise as an army's major assets. Scorning equipment, capitalizing on the fact that their numbers were small anyway, they put much more emphasis on surprise attack than on solid defense. They operated in the manner of the romantic Chinese bandits of Mao's favorite novel, *All Men Are Brothers,* a kind of Chinese Robin Hood story. Indeed, many of Mao's soldiers had once been bandits. Travelling light, with only their contacts and their courage to bolster them, the Red soldiers seemed freer and more humane than the average Chinese stereotype of a soldier. They retreated in the face of danger, but they were at least around for the next encounter. Mao himself told an American journalist that one of his heroes was George Washington, and that the reason he admired him was that Washington was a good guerrilla fighter, and one too stubborn to know enough to give up.

It was during the Ching Kang Shan period that Mao Tse-tung emerged as the Party's ideological, military and political leader. The son of a wily middle-class peasant, he had long believed in the revolutionary potential of the farmer. He had had unusually tempestuous relations with his father, in part at least over the issue of his father's exploitation of his farm workers. Mao had long counseled the Party to concentrate on peasants as well as industrial workers in building up its membership in China. Peasants were considered ignorant and conservative. Thus Mao's ideas were hard to fit into Marxist theory, and were ignored and laughed at for years.

In 1930, however, the Party was desperate. Most of its leaders were forced to admit that the "rising tide of revolution" which Marxist theory had promised was simply not happening among Chinese workers. They were rapidly becoming bourgeois, hopeful, and complacent, while in the countryside, poverty and anguish mounted. Why not turn to the peasants, Mao reasoned, and create an agricultural communism? He formed a soviet in the Hunan-Kiangsi border region where land was seized from the owners and redistributed so that everyone had a more equal share. It was the peasants who were affected. The "proletariat" was still favored on paper (there being several prestigious-sounding labor committees),but there were few workers in those isolated mountains.

Mao's rise to power was neither swift nor easy. Since he was unorthodox, he encountered resistance even in his own party, especially when the Central Committee joined him in Kiangsi after being forced out of Shanghai in 1932. Mao had two major Communist rivals. One was Chu Teh, the military leader who eventually agreed to support Mao's political aims, thus putting "politics in command" over the military in the Ching Kang Shan area. The other was Chou En-lai, whose political fortunes were hurt by his close alliance with Moscow and the "putschist line." Chou was also at a disadvantage in any quest for leadership because he had been a Shanghai theoretician while Mao had been gathering political power and soldiers in the mountains. Chou also acceded to Mao's leadership, acting with his lifelong grace in a powerful but secondary position. The fact that Mao was able to make loyal supporters out of each of these different men, and many others, attests to his charisma as well as his ruthlessness. At the same time it attests to a fierce commitment to their faltering cause felt by all three leaders.

Another substantial enemy for Mao was Chiang K'ai-shek, who, suddenly realizing what was happening in the mountains, circled the Communists' stronghold in the early thirties, and, with the help of a Nazi military planner, sent five "extermination campaigns" against them. This kind of fighting was what Sun Wu had warned against, and the Communists, in spite of heroic resistance in the beginning, were massively outnumbered. They were in touch with Moscow only by radio, and by late 1934 their fortunes were very low indeed.

At this point 100,000 Communists in the Ching Kang Shan area, men, women and children, undertook a daring and brilliantly managed expedition. It was called the Long March, and it *was* long, both in miles (more than 5,000) and in time (a year). Breaking out of Chiang's encircling armies in an isolated and unlikely place, they zigged and zagged across much of southwestern China, sometimes completely reversing their direction, in a frantic effort to avoid the KMT armies and at the same time eventually reach an area in northwestern China where they could rebuild their base. Twenty-four rivers were crossed, eighteen mountain ranges, areas where the people were hostile, areas of famine. Most amazing of all, the Communists' daring, courage, good manners, self-control, and, most of all, their success, made the Long March the most effective travelling propaganda show in history. All kinds of people

Mao Tse-tung on the Long March

who had never heard of the Communists or their ideas were now confronting them personally, watching the shows which the Communists put on at nearly every stop. Many were impressed by what they saw. Travelling mostly at night, many Communists were killed, yet they survived so many hard times and outfoxed the KMT at so many turns that they were considered the victors.

Mao proved himself to be tough. He survived illness, the strafing of his wife, and the harsh necessity of placing his two sons with a peasant family found along the route. He showed much of the same stubbornness and stamina as he had admired in Washington. After the first few defeats, he prevailed upon the others to abandon the heaviest wagons and simply live without the various "necessities" they had carried. Most important of all, the Communists were now totally out of contact with Moscow, so it was during this march that even the most die-hard Russian-trained dogmatists had to acknowledge Mao's dominance over the communist movement in China.

They landed eventually in an area in Shensi where soviets had already been set up. It was a desolate part of the country, relatively free of Chiang's control, sparsely populated, with abandoned caves to restore and land to terrace on the dusty loess hillsides. Government was immediately set in motion again, once more stressing opportunities for the poor, land redistribution, greater education, and a Red Army which planted crops instead of looting larders.

It also emphasized resistance to the Japanese, who by 1937 ostensibly occupied much of eastern China. Since Japan's hold over China was only in the cities and the railways, the Communist guerrillas could easily move around at night, doing damage to the railways and making contacts in the villages. Although they were committing only small amounts of men and materiel, they were well-known, keeping the war going, and encouraging Chinese patriots all over the world. They were also extending their own influence over the areas in north central China in which they worked behind the lines. In the name of resistance, the CCP built up their armies, planted Party workers, and engaged in a slow, steady propaganda barrage aimed at raising the political consciousness of the Chinese peasant. The war made it easy to get the peasant to listen.

As Chiang moved to Chungking and grew more militarized and conservative, large numbers of intellectuals joined Mao's cause or became sympathetic to it.* Anger at the Japanese became linked with anger at the government which seemed to be doing so little to

*One was a Shanghai actress, Chiang Ching, who arrived in Yenan while Mao's wife was in Moscow having her wounds attended. Soon afterwards, Chiang Ching became Mao's third wife.

protect its citizens. Thus it was that the Communists, whose ideological roots were foreign and class-based, came to seem more nationalistic than the Nationalists.

The "Yenan Period," like the Long March, is still celebrated and idealized in Chinese Communist memory and literature, music and woodcuts. Mao lived simply in a cave like everyone else's, with the same amount of food, the same kind of mosquito netting. What set him apart from others was the length of his workday, the endurance of his energy and commitment, and the extent of his accomplishments. After a long day's work, he would undertake a long night's writing, sometimes poetry, mostly political theory. Some of his most famous writing was done during the Yenan years.

During 1937 the Communists entered another "United Front" truce with the KMT. Like the earlier one, it had only one aim, the achievement of a short-term objective to force the withdrawal of Japan from Chinese territory. There was little or no intention on either side to enter into a longer term alliance or any form of real coordination. As a result of the agreement, the Communists ostensibly put their army, renamed the Eighth Route Army, under the control of the National Government. In fact, the KMT wasn't controlling much more than the southwest, so that the CCP, tied down on paper, was unhindered in practice. The Red Army became the real power in the countryside of northern China, making alliances with many separately organized resistance groups. As time went by, governments called "Border Regions" were set up which ruled vast areas which the CCP had never controlled before.

As the war progressed, these "liberated areas" spread outward from Yenan. In a few, social programs emphasized Mao's beliefs and gained the CCP experience and support among the peasants. Once the army was established in an area, the Party techniques began. The peasant was encouraged to participate in local decisions, rents which the landlords could collect from their tenants were reduced, and arrangements were made for the cooperative tackling of certain large projects. During this period, violence was avoided and order was restored. A small degree of prosperity returned, making the ordinary citizen much more willing to cooperate with the army as a sort of part-time guerrilla soldier should either the Japanese or the Kuo Min Tang return to the area.

Although control over the areas which were "liberated" was loose at first, and depended on persuasion as much as force, within the Party itself strict orthodoxy was the rule. Mao now set about to adjust Marxism-Leninism to Chinese conditions. He de-emphasized the doctrine that only the worker could successfully run a communist state. In fact, he said, many classes could share that load; peasants, workers, even intellectuals would have something to contribute. But all would be expected to work toward the one goal of classlessness, of strict equality between persons in a society. Certain classes had such an exploitative record that they would have to be watched carefully and deprived of responsibility, at least for a while. But after a process called "thought reform," when they understood what a better life the revolution could bring to all people, they too would be able to return to society.

This reasonableness and ability to compromise on matters of dogma was coupled with a vigilance and a messianic fervor in his own personality. Both seemed attractive to the Chinese people, and a large cult grew up around him. He was perceived as a good man, at home among peasants and able to listen to them, a fatherly figure who would love and protect his children, not only against foreigners, but also against poverty. Although the liberation he promised would be gained at the expense of nearly all one's personal freedom, most of the Chinese peasants, desperate for attention and material improvement, were willing to give it a try.

By the end of the Second World War, although both Mao and Chiang stated that their differences could be resolved politically rather than militarily, tensions were great between the two forces, and there had even been some battles between them. Each side had "atrocities" to report. Complicating China's problems was the Cold War between the USA and the USSR. Ignorant of or overlooking Mao's troubles with Russia and fierce sense of ideological independence, the U.S. policy makers assumed that any gain for the Communists in China was a Russian gain, and therefore an American loss. This reasoning led the Americans into the frail and unloving arms of Chiang K'ai-shek. Several diplomats who suggested that the U.S. might be wiser to support unity and cooperation rather than Chiang were accused of being "fellow-travellers" and drummed out of the service.

In spite of joint promises to American diplomats that a political compromise could be worked out, both sides were eager for a showdown. The Nationalists, with superior firepower supplied by the U.S., were afraid that time would bring the Communists advantages and they therefore initiated confrontation with the Communists in Manchuria in 1946. The Communists, using different military tactics requiring more speed and popular support but fewer arms, were also ready for the fight. They suspected that the

Nationalists were overconfident. What arms they did need were supplied by the Russians out of Manchurian stocks, and particularly were they afraid of losing the momentum which had been gained in the war.

The KMT strategy was to hold the cities defensively, but it was in the cities that their disastrous economic policies lost them support. Corruption and desertion, those two major enemies of any army, seemed to be everywhere. The Nationalists, trying by force and even assassination to prevent physical and ideological desertion only made things worse. The Chinese began asking the old Confucian question, "If one cannot 'govern by goodness,' should one be governing at all?"

The final confrontation between the two archenemies came in 1948 in the area just west of Shantung, an area rich in bandits and rebels all through Chinese history. Nationalist forces were cut off, short of supplies, lacking air protection, and directed by squabbling generals. Chiang insisted on second-guessing his generals, but by then he had lost the military shrewdness of his earlier days. Slowly and surely the tightly organized Communists were able to use their contacts among the peasants, their numbers and their complete ideological unity and military obedience to surround the Nationalist Army, cut off parts of it, and push the rest of it back until 130,000 men had been squeezed into only six square miles. This hardly gave them fighting room. When defeat was certain, more than half of the soldiers surrendered, a sure sign of the army's demoralization.

The late 1948 battle had involved one-fourth of Chiang's soldiers, and after their loss and capture the KMT's spirit was broken. All through 1949 different cities surrendered to the Communist forces: Tientsin and Peking in January, Shanghai in May, Canton in October, Chungking in November. Chiang and his followers were forced to take refuge again, this time from their fellow Chinese. And this time they went east, not west – to Taiwan.

The Military Principles of the Sun-tzu

Know yourself, and know your opponents, and in a hundred battles there will be a hundred victories.

If you plan the movement of your troops well, they will do what you did not even plan.

War is nothing but lies.

Be as swift as the wind, as secret as the forest, as consuming as fire, as silent as the mountains, as impenetrable as darkness, as sudden as thunderbolts.

We advance, and he cannot resist: for we strike where there is only emptiness. We retire and he cannot pursue, for we are too quick for him to reach us. When we wish to fight, though the enemy may be ensconced behind high walls and deep moats, he will have to give battle because we attack a place that he must assist. So we locate him, but he does not locate us, and we keep together while the enemy is defenseless.

Since we are many and the enemy few, and we can easily attack few, our victory will be easy: for the place where we give battle will be unknown, and being unknown, the enemy will have to prepare in many places. So it is that victory is a thing we make ourselves.

When discipline exists, disorder may be simulated; when there is courage, timidity may be simulated; when there is strength, weakness may be simulated.

The best plan is to strike at his war-plan, the next is to strike at his communications, the next is to strike at his armies, and the worst of all is to strike at his strongholds.

Nothing is to be gained by numbers.

From Robert Payne, *Mao Tse-tung: Ruler of Red China,* (New York, 1967), pp. 109-110.

The Heroes of Tatu.

The crossing of the Tatu River was the most critical single incident of the Long March. Had the Red Army failed there, quite possibly it would have been exterminated. The historic precedent for such a fate already existed. On the banks of the remote Tatu the heroes of the *Three Kingdoms* and many warriors since then had met defeat, and in these same gorges the last of the T'ai-p'ing rebels, an army of 100,000 led by Prince Shih Ta-k'ai, was in the nineteenth century surrounded and completely destroyed by the Manchu forces under the famous Tseng Kuo-fan. To warlords Liu Hsiang and Liu Wen-hui, his allies in Szechuan, and to his own generals in command of the government pursuit, Generalissimo Chiang now wired an exhortation to repeat the history of the T'ai-p'ing.

But the Reds also knew about Shih Ta-k'ai, and that the main cause of his defeat had been a costly delay. Arriving at the banks of the Tatu, Prince Shih had paused for three days to honor the birth of his son – an imperial prince. Those days of rest had given his enemy the chance to concentrate against him, and to make the swift marches in his rear that blocked his line of retreat. Realizing his mistake too late, Prince Shih had tried to break the enemy encirclement, but it was impossible to maneuver in the narrow terrain of the defiles, and he was erased from the map.

The Reds determined not to repeat his error. Moving rapidly northward from the Gold Sand River (as the Yangtze there is known) into Szechuan, they soon entered the tribal country of warlike aborigines, the "White" and "Black" Lolos of Independent Lololand. Never conquered, never absorbed by the Chinese who dwelt all around them, the turbulent Lolos had for centuries occupied that densely forested and mountainous spur of Szechuan whose borders are marked by the great southward arc described by the Yangtze just east of Tibet. Chiang Kai-shek could well have confidently counted on a long delay and weakening of the Reds here which would enable him to concentrate north of the Tatu. The Lolos' hatred of the Chinese was traditional, and rarely had any Chinese army crossed their borders without heavy losses or extermination.

But the Reds had already safely passed through the tribal districts of the Miao and the Shan peoples, aborigines of Kweichow and Yunnan, and had won their friendship and even enlisted some tribesmen in their army. Now they sent envoys ahead to parley with the Lolos. On the way they captured several towns on the borders of independent Lololand, where they found a number of Lolo chieftains who had been imprisoned as hostages by provincial Chinese warlords. Freed and sent back to their people, these men naturally praised the Reds.

In the vanguard of the Red Army was Commander Liu Po-ch'eng, who had once been an officer in a warlord army of Szechuan. Liu knew the tribal people, and their inner feuds and discontent. Especially he knew their hatred of Chinese, and he could speak something of the Lolo tongue. Assigned the task of negotiating a friendly alliance, he entered their territory and went into conference with the chieftains. The Lolos, he said, opposed warlords Liu Hsiang and Liu Wen-hui and the Kuomintang; so did the Reds. The Lolos wanted to preserve their independence; Red policies favored autonomy for all the national minorities of China. The Lolos hated the Chinese because they had been oppressed by them; but there were "White" Chinese and "Red" Chinese, just as there were "White" Lolos and "Black" Lolos, and it was the White Chinese who had always slain and oppressed the Lolos. Should not the Red Chinese and the Black Lolos unite against their common enemies, the White Chinese? The Lolos listened interestedly. Slyly they asked for arms and bullets to guard their independence and help Red Chinese fight the Whites. To their astonishment, the Reds gave them both.

And so it happened that not only a speedy but a politically useful passage was accomplished. Hundreds of Lolos enlisted with the "Red" Chinese to march to the Tatu River to fight the common enemy. Some of those Lolos were to trek clear to the Northwest. Liu Po-ch'eng drank the blood of a newly killed chicken before the high chieftain of the Lolos, who drank also, and they swore blood brotherhood in the tribal manner. By this vow the Reds declared that whosoever should violate the terms of their alliance would be even as weak and cowardly as the fowl.

Thus a vanguard division of the First Army Corps, led by Lin Piao, reached the Tatu Ho. On the last day of the march they emerged from the forests of Lololand (in the thick foliage of which Nanking pilots had completely lost track of them), to descend suddenly on the river town of An Jen Ch'ang, just as unheralded as they had come into Chou P'ing Fort. Guided over narrow mountain trails by the Lolos, the vanguard crept quietly up to the little town and from the heights looked down to the river bank, and saw with amazement and delight one of the three ferryboats made fast on the *south* bank of the river! Once more an act of fate had befriended them.

How had it happened? On the opposite shore there was only one regiment of the troops of General Lin Wen-hui, the co-dictator of Szechuan province. Other Szechuan troops, as well as reinforcements from Nanking, were leisurely proceeding toward the Tatu, but the single regiment meanwhile must have seemed enough. A squad should have been ample, with all boats moored to the north. But the commander of that regiment was a native of the district; he knew the country the Reds must pass through, and how long it would take them to penetrate to the river. They would be many days yet, he could have told his men. And his wife, one learned, had been a native of An Jan Ch'ang, so he must cross to the south bank to visit his relatives and his friends and to feast with them. Thus it happened that the Reds, taking the town by surprise, captured the commander, his boat, and their passage to the north.

Sixteen men from each of five companies volunteered to cross in the first boat and bring back the others, while on the south bank the Reds set up machine guns on the mountainsides and over the river spread a screen of protective fire concentrated on the enemy's exposed positions. It was May. Floods poured down the mountains, and the river was swift and even wider than the Yangtze. Starting far upstream, the ferry took two hours to cross and land just opposite the town. From the south bank the villagers of An Jen Ch'ang watched breathlessly. They would be wiped out! But wait. They saw the voyagers land almost beneath the guns of the enemy. Now, surely, they would be finished. And yet . . . from the south bank the Red machine guns barked on. The onlookers saw the little party climb ashore, hurriedly take cover, then slowly work their way up a steep cliff overhanging the enemy's positions. There they set up their own light machine guns and sent a downpour of lead and hand grenades into the enemy redoubts along the river.

Suddenly the White troops ceased firing, broke from their redoubts, and fled to a second and then a third line of defense. A great murmur went up from the south bank and shouts of *"Hao!"* drifted across the river to the little band who had captured the ferry landing. Meanwhile the first boat returned, towing two others, and on the second trip each carried eighty men. The enemy had fled. That day and night, and the next, and the next, those three ferries of An Jen Ch'ang worked back and forth, until at last nearly a division had been transferred to the northern bank.

But the river flowed faster and faster. The crossing became more and more difficult. On the third day it took four hours to shift a boatload of men from shore to shore. At this rate it would be weeks before the whole army and its animals and supplies could be moved. Long before the operation was completed they would be encircled. The First Army Corps had now crowded into An Jen Ch'ang, and behind were the flanking columns, and the transport and rear guard. Chiang Kai-shek's airplanes had found the spot, and heavily bombed it. Enemy troops were racing up from the southeast; others approached from the north. A hurried military conference was summoned by Lin Piao. Chu Teh, Mao Tse-tung, Chou En-lai, and P'eng Teh-huai had by now reached the river. They took a decision and began to carry it out at once.

Some 400 *li* to the west of An Jen Ch'ang, where the gorges rise very high and the river flows narrow, deep, and swift, there was an iron-chain suspension bridge called the Liu Ting Chiao – the Bridge Fixed by Liu. It was the last possible crossing of the Tatu east of Tibet. Toward this the barefoot Reds now set out along a trail that wound through the gorges, at times climbing several thousand feet, again dropping low to the level of the swollen stream itself and wallowing through waist-deep mud. If they captured the Liu Ting Chiao the whole army could enter central Szechuan. If they failed they would have to retrace their steps through Lololand, re-enter Yunnan, and fight their way westward toward Likiang, on the Tibetan border – a detour of more of than a thousand *li,* which few might hope to survive.

As their main forces pushed westward along the southern bank, the Red division already on the northern bank moved also. Sometimes the gorges between them closed so narrowly that the two lines of Reds could shout to each other across the stream; sometimes that gulf between them measured their fear that the Tatu might separate them forever, and they stepped more swiftly. As they wound in long dragon files along the cliffs at night their 10,000 torches sent arrows of light slanting down the dark face of the imprisoning river. Day and night these vanguards moved at double-quick, pausing only for brief ten-minute rests and meals, when the soldiers listened to lectures by their weary political workers, who over and over again explained the importance of this one action, exhorting each to give his last breath, his last urgent strength, for victory in the test ahead of them. There could be no slackening of pace, no halfheartedness, no fatigue. "Victory was life," said P'eng Teh-huai; "defeat was certain death."

On the second day the vanguard on the right bank fell behind. Szechuan troops had set up positions in the road, and skirmishes took place. Those on the southern bank pressed on more grimly. Presently new troops appeared on the opposite bank, and through their field glasses the Reds saw that they were White reinforcements, hurrying to the Bridge Fixed by Liu. For a whole day these troops raced each other along the stream, but gradually the Red vanguard, the pick of all the Red Army, pulled away from the enemy's tired soldiers, whose rests were longer and more frequent, whose energy seemed more spent, and who were perhaps none too anxious to die for a bridge.

The Bridge Fixed by Liu was built centuries ago, and in the manner of all bridges of the deep rivers of western China. Sixteen heavy iron chains, with a span of some 100 yards or more, were stretched across the river, their ends imbedded on each side under great piles of cemented rock, beneath the stone bridgeheads. Thick boards lashed over the chains made the road of the bridge, but upon their arrival the Reds found that half this wooden flooring had been removed, and before them only the bare iron chains swung to a point midway in the stream. At the northern bridgehead an enemy machine-gun nest faced them, and behind it were positions held by a regiment of White troops. The bridge should, of course, have been destroyed, but the Szechuanese were sentimental about their few bridges; it was not easy to rebuild them, and they were costly. Of Liu Ting it was said that "the wealth of the eighteen provinces contributed to build it." And who would have thought the Reds would insanely try to cross on the chains alone? But that was what they did.

No time was to be lost. The bridge must be captured before enemy reinforcements arrived. Once more volunteers were called for. One by one Red soldiers stepped forward to risk their lives, and, of those who offered themselves, thirty were chosen. Hand grenades and Mausers were strapped to their backs, and soon they were swinging out above the boiling river, moving hand over hand, clinging to the iron chains. Red machine guns barked at enemy redoubts and spattered the bridgehead with bullets. The enemy replied with machine-gunning of his own, and snipers shot at the Reds tossing high above the water, working slowly toward them. The first warrior was hit, and dropped into the current below; a second fell, and then a third. But as others drew nearer the center, the bridge flooring somewhat protected these dare-to-dies, and most of the enemy bullets glanced off, or ended in the cliffs on the opposite bank.

Probably never before had the Szechuanese seen fighters like these – men for whom soldiering was not just a rice bowl, and youths ready to commit suicide to win. Were they human beings or madmen or gods? Was their own morale affected? Did they perhaps not shoot to kill? Did some of them secretly pray that these men would succeed in their attempt? At last one Red crawled up over the bridge flooring, uncapped a grenade, and tossed it with perfect aim into the enemy redoubt. Nationalist officers ordered the rest of the planking torn up. It was already too late. More Reds were crawling into sight. Paraffin was thrown on the planking, and it began to burn. By then about twenty Reds were moving forward on their hands and knees, tossing grenade after grenade into the enemy machine-gun nest.

Suddenly, on the southern shore, their comrades began to shout with joy. "Long live the Red Army! Long live the Revolution! Long live the heroes of Tatu Ho!" For the enemy was withdrawing in pell-mell flight. Running full speed over the remaining planks of the bridge, through the flames licking toward them, the assailants nimbly hopped into the enemy's redoubt and turned the abandoned machine gun against the shore.

More Reds now swarmed over the chains, and arrived to help put out the fire and replace the boards. And soon afterwards the Red division that had crossed at An Jen Ch'ang came into sight, opening a flank attack on the remaining enemy positions, so that in a little while the White troops were wholly in flight – either in flight, that is, or with the Reds, for about a hundred Szechuan soldiers here threw down their rifles and turned to join their pursuers. In an hour or two the whole army was joyously tramping and singing its way across the River Tatu into Szechuan. Far overhead angrily and impotently roared the planes of Chiang Kai-shek, and the Reds cried out in delirious challenge to them.

For their distinguished bravery the heroes of An Jen Ch'ang and Liu Ting Chiao were awarded the Gold Star, highest decoration in the Red Army of China.

Edgar Snow, *Red Star Over China*, (Grove Press, Inc.), pp. 194-199.

Quotations of Chairman Mao

In class society everyone lives as a member of a particular class, and every kind of thinking, without exception, is stamped with the brand of a class.

Changes in society are due chiefly to the development of the internal contradictions in society, that is, the contradiction between the productive forces and the relations of production, the contradiction between classes and the contradiction between the old and the new; it is the development of these contradictions that pushes society forward and gives the impetus for the supersession of the old society by the new.

Communism is at once a complete system of proletarian ideology and a new social system. It is different from any other ideological and social system, and is the most complete, progressive, revolutionary and rational system in human history. The ideological and social system of feudalism has a place only in the museum of history. The ideological and social system of capitalism has also become a museum piece in one part of the world (in the Soviet Union), while in other countries it resembles a "dying person who is sinking fast, like the sun setting beyond the western hills," and will soon be relegated to the museum. The communist ideological and social system alone is full of youth and vitality, sweeping the world with the momentum of an avalanche and the force of a thunderbolt.

Every Communist must grasp the truth, "Political power grows out of the barrel of a gun."

If anyone attacks us and if the conditions are favorable for battle, we will certainly act in self-defense to wipe him out resolutely, thoroughly, wholly and completely (we do not strike rashly, but when we do strike, we must win). We must never be cowed by the bluster of reactionaries.

The rise of the present peasant movement is a colossal event. In a very short time, in China's central, southern and northern provinces, several hundred million peasants will rise like a tornado or tempest, a force so extraordinarily swift and violent that no power, however great, will be able to suppress it. They will break all trammels that now bind them and rush forward along the road to liberation. They will send all imperialists, warlords, corrupt officials, local bullies and bad gentry to their graves.

142

With the fall of the authority of the landlords, the peasant association becomes the sole organ or authority, and what people call "All power to the peasant association" has come to pass. Even such a trifle as a quarrel between man and wife has to be settled at the peasant association. Nothing can be settled in the absence of people from the association. The association is actually dictating in all matters in the countryside, and it is literally true that "whatever it says, goes."

Poetry Written by Mao Tse-Tung

LIUPENG MOUNTAIN

The sky is high, the clouds are winnowing,
I gaze southwards at the wild geese disappearing over the horizon.
I count on my fingers, a distance of twenty thousand *li*.
I say we are not heroes if we do not reach the Great Wall.
Standing on the highest peak of Six Mountains,
The red flag streaming in the west wind,
Today with a long rope in my hand,
I wonder how soon before we can bind up the monster.

THE LONG MARCH

No one in the Red Army fears the hardships of the Long March.
We looked lightly on the thousand peaks and the ten thousand
    rivers.
The Five Mountains rose and fell like rippling waves,
The Wu Meng Mountains were no more than small green pebbles.
Warm were the sheer precipices when Gold Sand River dashed into
    them,
Gold were the iron-chained bridges over the Tatu River.
Delighting in the thousand snowy folds of the Min Mountains,
The last pass vanquished, the Three Armies smiled.

From Robert Payne, *Mao Tse-Tung: Ruler of Red China,* 1967, pp. 230-231.

Street scene in Modern China

9

Extending Party
Control: 1949-1961

The Communist takeover in China was only the beginning of major changes. Between wars and campaigns, revolutions and detentes, and through all kinds of shifts in the "mass line" – what the Party called the government's view of the correct ideas at any given moment – the Chinese since 1949 have constantly been in a state of transition. This was as Mao planned it, namely that the first generation after "liberation" should be spent in "readying the people for socialism." During this time, he expected a "vanguard" of the most experienced and able Communists to make the people see that their lives and fortunes were truly tied to a successful socialist state. In theory, after they saw this, they could take over for themselves. It was political tutelage as Sun Yat-sen had described it, except that the elite group Sun envisioned was drawn out of the educated upper class. Mao's elite would ideally have been made up of persons from the lowest and thus most revolutionary classes, and their training would have consisted of participation in the Revolution rather than study.

The shifting relationship between the leaders and the led, between the vanguard and the people, was troubling for Mao, as it is for any leader under any political system. The danger is that the vanguard will forget the temporary nature of its mission. Yet if one tries to govern without an elite, how will one manage? Will the factories run smoothly, will technologies be developed, will the people retain their hard-won unity? How can the state gain the benefits of a hard-working elite without paying a price? All of these questions troubled Mao from the moment he came to power.

Mao had to achieve at least two aims or he would not keep the "mandate" which he wanted. First, he wanted to make China socialistic: that is, all property, whether land, money or possessions, would have to be more and more tied to the public, rather than the private, interest. Second, he wanted to show that the newer and more egalitarian (and state-controlled) arrangement of property would "unleash the energies of the people," and thus

145

lead to greater productivity and a higher standard of living. Like Mencius, Mao believed that goodness in men comes only when they have had enough to eat. Thus, if one wanted to make a man into a more charitable and community-oriented person, one must start by improving the simple things about his own life such as how well he eats, how large and in how good repair his house is, whether he can read, whether he is cared for when he is sick.

The problem with these twin aims, the development of the people's economic welfare and of their commitment to a socialistic society both at the same time, is that they often tug against each other. Mao could call it "walking on two legs," but the simple fact was that the improvement of the people's standard of living required industrialization to increase efficiency, and industrialization required having knowledgeable, take-charge types, experts, to direct a delicate and complex process. But could there be room for experts in a society which had declared itself against hierarchy?

The answer which Mao seems to have given to this question is "sometimes." Sometimes there's room for experts, sometimes there isn't. This seemed to have solved the problem to his satisfaction. His twining and intertwining of these two threads, socialization and industrialization, reds and experts, made the old dynastic cycles look like simple stuff.

When reviewing the twenty-seven years of Mao's regime, these shifting attitudes are apparent. Back and forth went his emphases; almost always, China seemed to be walking more on one leg than on the other, but *which* leg constantly shifted! The one constant in this confusing scene was the increase of Mao's domination over China.

In 1949, Mao was faced with a country ravaged by twelve years of war, a tremendous inflation, and desperate poverty. His own followers were too inexperienced and too small in number to lead the nation out of this quagmire. He therefore resolved to go slowly at first, treading only lightly on the toes of the intellectuals and the bourgeoisie. Although Mao was ardent about getting rid of the Kuo Min Tang and any active sympathizers it might still command, he felt in 1949 that the job had been largely done. Major landowners and the very wealthy had been mostly "identified by the people" in that they had either been killed right in the villages (thus letting the peasants take part directly in the Revolution) or else jailed or chased away. Now that the war was over, Mao extended his arms broadly to all social classes to work together and share power. His statement on the subject, "On the People's Democratic Dictatorship," proposed that the peasantry and bourgeoisie be allowed to keep small plots of privately owned land, as long as they were working for the good of all of the Chinese. Experts would be respected and welcomed. They were put to work in big jobs during the early 1950's. Many of the government workers who had worked for the KMT were kept at their jobs. Mao kept the right to isolate "enemies of the people" wherever he found them, but at first he didn't find many.

In an effort to get the economy moving, Mao devised several clever schemes for battling the inflation. He first reduced spending by controlling it. No longer could corruption dominate an area's economy. He then taxed both manufactured and agricultural goods in order to raise more revenue for the government. Since the currency situation was out of control, a new and temporary currency was issued. Value was determined in units of what-could-be-bought rather than the old names of the currency. This tended to stabilize things, and it gave the people enough confidence to revive the old pre-war market items. They began to leave their homes, even their villages, and do a little trading in the market towns.

Mao made sure that manufacturing developed in the way he wanted by controlling both credit and raw materials. Heavy industry, railroads, and foreign trade were all brought under state control. The peasant-based Party decided initially to invest heavily in the cities, and tried to rebuild the Manchurian industrial base which had been built up by the Japanese and then destroyed by the war or removed by the Russians. As railroads were repaired and the inflation was controlled, more trade began to take place between regions. The improvement in the economy not only somewhat eased China's distress but brought much new confidence in Mao's leadership.

As for political control, the Communists were determined to reach a higher proportion of the Chinese people than the Kuo Min Tang had done, to teach them how to live in a socialist society, and to gain their understanding and support. To accomplish these objectives, they took the levels of governing bodies all the way down to the villages. They set up massive Regional and National Congresses which had little power but nonetheless official-sounding functions. Like the old imperial system, the Congresses and government workers were much busier representing the central power to the people than the people to the government power. The Communists called the process "democratic centralism," the democratic part meaning that all classes were represented, and the centralized part indicating that a few men in the center were making nearly all of the decisions. The people, at any rate, were already used to that sort of government in China.

Besides the specific governmental lifeline, the Communists set up mass organizations for women, for youth, for students, even for the "National Bourgeoisie." These organizations were partly political, partly social in nature, involving meetings, study programs, welfare work, street committees (reminiscent of the old *pao chia* system) and constant explanation and re-explanation of the "mass line." In other words, through these organizations a person was in some way reached by the Party, and at one point half of the Chinese population was in one or another of these organizations. What a change from the old days of the politically apathetic Chinese peasant!

It was through the mass organizations that the "campaigns," or movements to attain one specific goal by the application of widespread energy, were started and gained momentum. The mechanics were already there, and the numbers were huge.

To set the Young Pioneers to cleaning streets, explaining cooperatives, or searching for "reactionaries" was to get the job done. One summer they were encouraged to rid Shanghai of all of its flies, and with much competition over who could bring more of their dead victims to school, they did it. The mass organizations, orchestrating many of these separate campaigns and movements, had become a formidable instrument. By remaining small itself, the Party retained its discipline. The mass organizations, however, gave it an impression of accessibility.

In addition to the political revolution, the Communist Party oversaw the final demise of the traditional social ethic. As we have seen, the end of certain Chinese institutions such as footbinding, the inferiority of women, the family as the chief economic unit, and the old family system, had been approaching for some time. Foreigners had long found some of the customs outlandish and had so stated. During the May Fourth Movement and the Nationalist era, many of the old customs were undermined and disappeared.

It took the new regime, however, to create a new marriage law in 1950 making women the legal equals of men. A series of campaigns encouraged children to reform and (in the most bitter cases) to report to the authorities any misdeeds of their parents. All this must have set Confucius spinning in his grave! The old family unit, which settled most of its own affairs, which shared in guilt and poverty and also in prosperity, was now to be replaced by the state. The loyalty once owed to one's family or clan would now be transferred to the larger social unit.

But how to do that? States are such distant and unlovable phenomena. Mao personalized the state in two ways. First, he allowed the local political and economic units, the collectives, some measure of real, and even more imagined, autonomy. They were quite small at first, the size of an extended family or a small village, in order that the member might feel quite comfortable identifying with the collective. Second, Mao allowed the "cult of Mao" to become more and more powerful. People everywhere looked at his picture, repeated his words and analyzed his actions. They sang songs about him, and relived his most famous adven-

Mao and his Wife, Chiang Ching

tures in their theatres. Discussing him several times a day, they felt very close to him, even though he was so far away. He was perceived as the ancient emperors had been perceived, as a good man. The opportunity to know a lot about him was much more possible for the twentieth-century Chinese person than it had been for his ancestors to know the emperor.

Another item in Mao's social program had to do with this spread of stories, articles and ideas. It was literacy. For the Communists, an increase in literacy meant a rise in general well-being, a rise in potential productivity, and also, and most important, a greater opportunity of reaching the Chinese people. No longer were they assembled to hear the same maxims read twice a month before the temple. The times moved too fast for that, but the message was still there and it was still controlled from above. More readers meant more people who would have direct exposure to Mao's words and the "mass line," without the dangerous interpretations which might be made on the local level. Reading enough about an event would make a person remember it as it was reported to be, rather than how he himself had actually experienced it. Literacy was a great boon, but it was also a powerful political instrument.

In his preoccupation with gaining widespread support, setting up workable political and social apparati, and controlling inflation, Mao had come to rely on experts, people who were useful to the regime and who wanted to be useful, but who were not yet ideological Communists in their hearts. All this changed during the Korean War. Although Mao had not encouraged the North Korean Communist state to attack the South, a 1950 defense treaty with Russia as well as Chinese concern about Manchuria led them to enter the war after the South Korean forces, bolstered by the United Nations, seemed to be gaining the upper hand. With Russian help, the Chinese troops, called "volunteers," were amazingly effective at holding the U.N. forces (mostly American) to a standstill. Further angering the Chinese was the U.S. Seventh Fleet, which prevented them from invading Taiwan and getting rid of Chiang once and for all. The Korean War hardened China's attitude toward the U.S., and led to closer dependence on Russia's friendship and arms.

At home in China during the war, a wave of anger and fear led the government to decide to crack down on all laggards, counter-revolutionaries and American sympathizers. The definition of the "enemies of the people" was widened considerably. Western-trained scholars, members of the "National Bourgeoisie" and many others who had gone under the rubric of expert were subjected to a process called "thought reform," in which they were questioned closely by Party members to find traces of sympathy with any causes but the CCP's. A combination of eagerness to feel at home in the new state, worry as one's friends and family supports were removed, and finally outright terror at what might be in store for the "deviate," led these suspected persons to profess complete loyalty to the state, give up to it their homes, possessions and promising careers, and emerge "new" men, "cleansed" of all their former "arrogance" and "individualism."

Besides thought reform, the years 1951 and 1952 brought the "Three Anti" (against "officialdom" in the government, the state industries and the Party) and the "Five Anti" (against bribery, tax evasion, theft of state assets, cheating in labor or materials, and stealing state economic intelligence) campaigns. All of these crimes were possible only for the insiders in a society, as one can't steal a state secret unless one has been entrusted with it or can gain easy access to it. Thus in many ways these "Three Anti" and "Five Anti" campaigns were directed against the very persons who had formerly been part of the vanguard. The National Bourgeoisie especially suffered. Huge amounts were taken from its members in fines, taxes and imprisonments, and as a class it was officially dead by 1956.

Dogmatic purity was also pursued in the landholding area. Up until 1952, land reform had meant a process of taking private lands away from the rich, dividing them up, and giving small private plots to the poor. By the end of 1952, the campaigns had given the Chinese leaders enough control over the country so that they felt that they could push for a more socialistic and efficient arrangement, namely, collectivization. Certain vast jobs such as dikes, bridges, motorized plowing, and forestry depended on the kind of space, resources and energy which no one man could muster. Work brigades had already collected manpower for these jobs and they had led to greater productivity and even a small rise in the standard of living. Now land, too, would be collected, owned and farmed in common. The campaign to collectivize farm lands began in late 1952, and, encouraged by the Party and by demonstrated success in some early examples, the peasants collectivized rapidly during the mid-fifties.

"Ownership" was at the collective, not the state level, making the farmers feel that the lands were still theirs. Although the "mass line" was inevitably followed, there was a feeling on the local level that it was their own discussions which had led them to desire greater socialization. The process of persuasion and reinforcement was constant, as there was usually an increase in a given area's productivity, and so material welfare. The Party sent back part of the collective's increased taxes in the form of new seeds, a new tractor, or government workers who organized local projects. Finally, if there were still dissidents, they were either eliminated or cowed. The peasants saw no alternative except to trust the word of their Chairman. By ridding the countryside of the landlords, he'd been good to them earlier; perhaps he would know best for them again. As one of them put it: "I decided . . . that I would first hear what the Party said and follow it and not argue. Because the Party had always been right before."*

*Jan Myrdal, *Report From a Chinese Village* (New York,1965), p. 91.

The push for collectivization was linked to the First Five Year Plan, which was set for the years 1953-1957. One of the purposes of collectivization was to make it easier to collect tax revenue, and this revenue was to become some of the capital needed to finance industrialization. The many advisors from Russia who were now in China, bringing with them equipment, loans and experience, urged this plan. But rapid industrialization and the build up of China's roads and railroads were the core of this plan, and they tended to give power back to the experts who had been sidelined back in the early fifties. The Party needed them, not only for their mechanical skills, but it also needed their inventiveness and curiosity. It was necessary for them to feel that both freedom of thought existed along with the opportunity to display individual talent and aptitude while working for the new China. The patriotic Mao even needed the experts to show the Russians that there was Chinese talent available to him, that he was not utterly dependent on Russian technical skills. It was in an effort to rescue the former intellectuals and reharness them to China's cause that Mao proclaimed his "One Hundred Flowers" campaign in 1956 and 1957. As part of this campaign, Mao encouraged more breadth of thought for the intellectuals, access to foreign publications, increase in higher education, more ability to add their particular talents and emphases to a common plan. He adopted an old Chinese saying for his slogan:

> "Let One Hundred Flowers Bloom!
> Let One Hundred Schools of Thought Contend!"

The analogy with blooming flowers was an apt one. Mao proclaimed that there was no kind of official flower, as different flowers could bloom successfully side by side. Yet there was no official approval of weeds, and the Party was still to decide what constituted a weed and what a blooming flower. Dandelions and goldenrod, beware! Thus, the Blooming Flowers Period, welcome respite though it was after years of emphasis on thought reform, did not go very far. The ability to criticize the Party cadres who had zealously stifled new ideas was always limited. The basic loyalty to the one-party state must never be in doubt. As an aftermath to the torrent of criticism which emerged during the Blooming Flowers Period, a new wave of arrests was made.

As "enemies of the people" these foolhardy intellectuals were not alone. The effort to liberate and at the same time harness the experts merged with a campaign to control the Party cadres, who had been showing dangerous signs of considering themselves a kind of permanent upper class. Attempting to "rectify this false working style," the Party began a policy of *hsia fang,* or "downward transfer," in which Party workers were sent to the countryside to "learn from the masses," regain humility and a sense of dependence on the Party, and incidentally to help to bring in the harvests. Mao produced a series of new statements on the limits of contradiction. As a peasant's son, he had always been suspicious of city people, and he began to doubt his former policy of building up the cities.

Finally in 1958 the Party called for what they termed a Great Leap Forward. Communes, which were larger and more varied than collectives, were set up. These would reflect the new spirit of industrialization, but at the same time they would decentralize China's industry and would promote socialism. The commune would also create a larger economic unit from which it would be easier to extract money and goods for the Party's industrialization efforts. To save womanpower, and further weaken the nuclear family, mess halls and day care centers were set up. Set wages and even work points were abandoned. Payment would be made according to need instead of according to work. Backyard plots in which a family might grow vegetables for themselves were forbidden. All economic and even most social activity was to be tied to the state.

In some senses the Great Leap Forward was like the earlier Five Year Plan, stressing the improvement of China's industrial capacity, even to the extent of catching up with Britain in that respect within fifteen years. The rise in industrial capacity, however, was not going to be achieved in the usual way, that is in large cities, where large capital was invested in large factories managed by large experts with large egos. No, Mao insisted, the Chinese were going to solve their industrialization problems in their own particularly ethnocentric, particularly socialistic way. He stressed the home-grown solution, the talent which could be found in the simplest of men, the ingenuity which only the Chinese peasant could bring to a problem. Watching progress all around him, the ordinary Chinese citizen would feel a surge of unseen energies and unsuspected talents drawn out of him in response.

The Great Leap Forward as an industrialization plan was entirely different from the one which large numbers of Russian advisors in China had been urging. They had supported the Five Year Plan, with its emphasis on careful planning and large-scale technical improvements. The Great Leap Forward threatened them with its decentralization, its vast plans, and Mao claimed, with its rapid jump into full-fledged socialism, achieving that phase more quickly and more completely than the Russians themselves had done. Over these issues the Russian-Chinese alliance was weakened, and in 1960 and 1961 many of the advisors went back to Russia. Years later, one of them, asked to comment on his years in China, simply shook his head. "Crazy," he said, "the whole lot of them are simply crazy."

Like the ancient Chinese Taoists, Mao now stressed more instinct, less education. His goals became romantic rather than realistic. The story about the "Old Man Who Could Move Mountains" became everyone's required reading. The "Half-Work Half-Study Schools" were a product of this stress on activism and problem-solving rather than on isolated study and planning. Biology would be studied only with local farming problems in mind, math was to be relevant, or else abandoned, and literature was all political in nature. The newspapers were full of stories about local triumphs: backyard smelters run by farmer-engineers, lands reclaimed by farmer-geochemists, seeds developed by farmer-biologists. There was much competition over who could devise the cleverest schemes, produce more, and then sacrifice more by sending the largest quotas to Peking. It was guerrilla warfare on the economy. And the Chinese were producing more, more, more every year.

Or were they? The extravagant reports and ambitious plans of 1958, which claimed that production had actually doubled in some areas, had to be revised in 1959. The eager cadres, no longer under centralized control, anxious to look loyal and productive, unskilled in statistics, had simply over-reported. They had, furthermore, squeezed too much out of the people. Nothing connected; there were no railroads to carry away the painfully produced perishable goods; there were no materials for a balanced economy or even a balanced diet in any of the separate sections. Making educated people into manual laborers and peasants into scientists might be exciting in the short term, but was it really practical in the long term sense? There was grumbling. And in addition, the steel made in the backyard furnaces had the embarrassing habit of developing holes and cracks.

Both emotion and money had been invested in the Great Leap Forward, and when it faltered, there were hard times in China. Poor harvests because of bad weather compounded the problem, and in 1960 and 1961 actual starvation occurred in some sections. The whole notion of private plots, discredited in any socialistic program, had to be permitted again, as did payment according to work rather than need. The mess halls were often given up. The Party had found that productivity was suffering from the new working style, and so once again there were more collectives in China than communes. The Great Leap Forward had in fact pulled China's economy substantially backward.

Description of Thought Reform

The interrogator made a gesture toward a short stool in the centre of the room. As I sat I noticed a piece of chalk placed carefully on the floor between the two front legs of the stool. The interrogator gazed contemplatively down at me and started from the beginning.

'Your name?'

'Bao Ruo-wang.'

'Your original name?'

'Pasqualini.'

'Take that piece of chalk and write it on the floor in big letters.'

So that's what it was for. The routine continued – address before arrest, employment, nationality . . . He went through the detail mechanically and with obvious boredom. He showed no signs of animation until he reached the point where he could begin making speeches. Interrogators are born speech-makers.

'Now then. Before we start, there are some things I have to tell you. The people in your cell have probably told you the government's policy toward those who are arrested for counter-revolutionary and political activities. Can you read Chinese?'

'No,' I admitted. Despite the fact that I spoke Mandarin like a native, I had never been taught to read or write it. That came later – in the camps. The interrogator pointed to the characters on a banner pinned to the wall. This was the official version, which he read off for me:

'Leniency to those who confess; severity to those who resist; redemption to those who obtain merits; rewards to those who gain big merits.'

I noticed the slight differences between this and the version Loo told me in the cell. Evidently he had done some embroidering.

'This is the government's policy,' the interrogator continued. 'It is the way to salvation for you. In front of you are two paths: the one of confessing everything and obeying the government, which will lead you to a new life, the other of resisting the orders of the government and stubbornly remaining the people's enemy right to the very end. This path will lead to the worst possible consequences. It is up to you to make the choice. The sooner you confess your crimes, the sooner you will go home. The better your confession, the quicker you will rejoin your wife and children.

'You need not worry about your family. The government will look after them. You are the guilty one, not they. The families of counterrevolutionaries are not discriminated against in any manner. If they are in difficulties, the government is there to help them. So set your heart at ease and confess your crimes thoroughly. If you behave properly, we might recommend you for leniency when the time comes for that. But if you show yourself to be stubborn and a die-hard imperialist without an ounce of regret, then the outcome is too frightful to contemplate. Do you understand me?'

I nodded. I was, in fact, very relieved by what he said about the government taking care of my family. It was good news at the time. Only later I learned that it was a lie – when I was in the camps, my wife and children were hungrier that I was.

'There are two types of confessions. We call them Toothpaste and Water Tap. The Toothpaste prisoner needs to be squeezed every now and then, or else he forgets to keep confessing. The Water Tap man needs one good, hard twist before he starts, but then everything comes out. You are a reasonable person, an intelligent person. I don't think we need to resort to persuasion. Do you understand me?'

Silence. I nodded again and waited for him to go on.

'Good. So we'll begin. Do you know why you were brought here?'

I made my first mistake. 'When I was arrested they told me that I was a counterrevolutionary.'

My interrogator leaned forward in his chair angrily.

'*Told* that you are a counterrevolutionary? You *are* a counterrevolutionary! You are a spy of the imperialists! No one tells you – it is a fact! You will have to be frank with us or things will go badly for you. Speak!'

I suppose it must have been the arrogance of his manner that briefly raised what was left of my hackles. I hadn't been inside long enough to realize that a prisoner has no defenses, no justification whatever. I committed the presumption of answering back. For the last time in China, I was a wise guy.

'How can I be a counterrevolutionary,' I asked, 'if I am not Chinese?'

He stared at me, dumbfounded for a tiny moment, then exploded in unfeigned rage.

'How dare you ask us questions? Your activities have brought damage to the revolution and have caused great losses to the government. You are a counterrevolutionary through and through. All your life you have engaged in activities against the Communist Party and against the people. We have proof of it – plenty of proof.'

He calmed himself quickly. 'Now we are going to start again from the beginning. You will tell us your history properly.'

'Where shall I begin?'

'Before the Liberation, when you started working for the American imperialists.'

I began the long list, from the Marines, the Signal Corps, the Associated Press, but the interrogator was showing increasing signs of impatient discomfort. He broke in.

'We are not asking for your biography. We know where you have been working. We have records for that. What we want is a confession of your crimes. You are giving us all these details but nothing about your crimes against the people. Do you realize what you are? You are an agent of the imperialists and a loyal running-dog of the Americans. Tell us all the dirty work you did for them. We have complete records in our files and we have formal accusations from people you victimized in the past. Tell us about your duties as interpreter for the Marine Military Police. Was interpretation the only work you did?'

It was easy to see what he was getting at. It was also easy to see I was in trouble. No matter how much I might try to minimize my role as interpreter, I couldn't avoid piling incriminations on my head. The Communists had always regarded the military police as an organization of repression against the Chinese people and as an intelligence-gathering agency. I had not only accepted their pay and their orders, but had quite willingly worked in the middle of all their activities – some of which were painful. I had been along on raids against blackmarket rings, confiscations, all sorts of vice-squad dealings, interrogations of civilians. I was well known. There were plenty of black marketeers, night club operators, pimps, whores and God knows what other characters who could have poured out their meretricious tales of suffering under the Americans, once the Communists were in power and puritanism became the call of the day. I began talking about the Marines and went on until half past noon, when he ordered me to stop and called for a guard to return me to the cell.

'How did it go?' Loo asked me.

'Well, I don't know. They told me I'd be called again.'

'Of course you'll be called again.' Loo spoke with the amused indulgence of a schoolmaster. 'Perhaps dozens of times. That is what we are here for – to be interrogated. Interrogation is a good thing. It is the solution of our problems and the settlement of our cases. The sooner we end the interrogations by being open and frank, the sooner we will leave here. You must make efforts to leave as soon as possible.'

That was something he didn't have to tell me twice. Loo was a very unsettling person, though. I was really liking him a lot by now, but it mystified me why in hell he talked like a Communist functionary. That was something that would be cleared up for me in time, step by step. My interrogation, it turned out, was to last a full fifteen months, at the end of which I, too, was speaking like Loo. And I was begging to be sent away to a labour camp. Life is strange, but the human mind stranger.

It doesn't take a prisoner long to lose his self-confidence. Over the years Mao's police have perfected their interrogation methods to such a fine point that I would defy any man, Chinese or not, to hold out against them. Their aim is not so much to make you invent nonexistent crimes, but to make you accept your ordinary life, as you led it, as rotten and sinful and worthy of punishment, since it did not concord with their own, the police's, conception of how a life should be led. The basis of their success is despair, the prisoner's perception that he is utterly and hopelessly and forever at the mercy of his jailers. He has no defense, since his arrest is absolute and unquestionable proof of his guilt. (During my years in prison I knew of a man who was in fact arrested by mistake – right name but wrong man. After a few months he had confessed all the crimes of the other. When the mistake was discovered, the prison authorities had a terrible time persuading him to go back home. He felt too guilty for that.) The prisoner has no trial, only a well-rehearsed ceremony that lasts perhaps half an hour; no consultation with lawyers; no appeal in the Western sense. I say in the Western sense because there actually is a possible appeal, but it is such a splendidly twisted, ironic caricature that it is worthy of the best talents of Kafka, Orwell or Joseph Heller. We shall see that later.

Very soon I realized that I could expect no help from any quarter. My wife was petrified with fear, poor and in danger of being locked up herself. At the time France had no diplomatic relations with People's China and the Quai d'Orsay certainly wasn't prepared to make any trouble over me. I was nothing more than a half-breed who happened to be holding a French passport by luck of birth. I was no Jenkins, and no one was going to war over my ear . . .

My brain was flailing away trying to get all this business straightened out when, unexpectedly, I was called for a second interrogation. Again, I was taken aback and unnerved. Why another session at 8 p.m.? Everyone had indicated that they always took a few extra days to digest the material from the first session. The only explanation I could find was that my output that morning had been completely unsatisfactory, and that they were planning to try again, from another angle. And how right I was. It was pitch dark when a cop – a new one this time, but with the same fat pistol – led me through the maze of passageways and corridors. My apprehension mounted as we crossed the big courtyard in silence, and it was an almost friendly sight when we came upon the green door marked '41st'. I barked out my name and trotted in, head down, aiming crablike for the stool in the corner.

'Don't sit down.' It was the interrogator who spoke. 'We're going somewhere else this time.'

I stood studying the floor for another five minutes before another Sepo came in. We trooped out en masse. This time I had the privilege of four guards and four big pistols. We pushed bravely off into the night, me blindly leading the way as always, left-right, left-right. We came up before a huge, three-story structure that I took to be some kind of administration building, then inside and across a big, sparsely furnished meeting hall. I found myself at the head of a flight of red brick steps, lit dimly and twisting steeply downward. Down I went, boots creaking behind me. An iron gate stopped us, but one of the guards came forward with a key. I could make out another set of steps, even darker, plunging into the penumbra. The walls were closer, too, barely the width of my shoulders. With each step the air seemed to grow damper, warmer and more sickly. I felt as if I were walking into a plague. My mouth was dry. I was scared as hell. At the end of it all was a wooden door sheathed in iron.

'Baogao!' someone ordered behind me. 'Report!'

I shouted out my name and the door flew open. Two men in blue padded uniforms were there to jerk me inside and at the same time lock my arms behind me. There were ten more little steps down, then an opening and then – I found myself in a torture chamber.

I don't think a person screams when he is terrified. The first instinct is to freeze up. It's not possible, I thought, it's not possible, but there was a tiger bench before me, just as bright as life. I contemplated it numbly and felt cold. A tiger bench is a simple device, really, just a sort of articulated board. The client is tied firmly in several places, and then the bench can be raised in many different and interesting ways. Eventually it is the hip bones that crack first, I have been told. Next to the bench were water and towels, indispensable accessories for that great classic, the water torture. The towel goes over the prisoner's face and the water is poured gently on it. The man suffocates or drowns. It is a handy little torture, because it is light and portable. It is a technique that was much in vogue during the war in Vietnam. I looked around and saw bamboo splinters and hammers, and even a set of chains heating over a coal fire. I think I would have sunk to the floor if the two cops weren't supporting me by my arms. His face a stone mask, the interrogator stepped up before me. The faithful scribe followed, notebook in hand. And finally, after a long theatrical pause, I discovered the truth of this routine.

'This is a museum,' he said. 'Don't be afraid. We wanted you to have a look at this place so you could see how the Nationalist reactionaries used to question their prisoners. Now we are living in a different era. We are in a socialist society, under the humane regime of Chairman Mao and the Chinese Communist Party. We do not use such crude and inhumane methods. People who resort to torture do so only because they are weaker than their victims. We, on the other hand, are stronger than you. We are certain of our superiority. And the methods we use are a hundred times more efficient than this.'

He looked over the room with disdain, looked back at me for a long moment, then ordered the guard: 'Take him away.'

Long Live Chairman Mao, I thought as I shuffled out. From that moment on, my interrogations started going smoothly.

The next time I saw the interrogator he had a bit of psychopolitical explaining for me.

'You see, Bao, the reason you became frightened when you saw our museum the other night was that your mind has been poisoned by imperialist propaganda. What we showed you was just our way of letting you know that it is only the criminal Chiang Kai-shek regime that ever used torture. Now that you have learned the lesson you will see that the only way for you is to confess. It saves so much time for you and me. And there are so many advantages.'

'What do you want me to confess?'

He looked pained. 'We don't tell people what to confess. If we did, it would be an accusation and not a confession. Don't you see that we are giving you a chance? We already know everything about you, Bao. We want you to confess only to give you the opportunity to obtain some leniency. If what you tell us tallies with what we already know, then I can give you my word that you will be leniently treated. But if you tell us only five or ten per cent, then you'll never go home.'

'Where do I begin?'

'There are many ways. Some people prefer to start with the most important things and then work their way down to the details. But most are the opposite – they start with the trifles and little by little work their way up to what is really important. You might say they try to save the best part for the last. That's all right with us. We know we will get it eventually. And then there are some people who suffer from loss of memory and can only talk about the most recent things; they don't seem to like to talk about their past. It's all up to you, Bao. We have lots of time. Only one thing: Don't try to make fools of us. I can promise you it won't work.'

I began the story of my life, from age eight onward. The interrogator hardly interrupted again and listened with complete attention. The scribe took it down in Chinese characters with admirable speed and precision. That session lasted six hours in all. As the sessions continued the gaps between them gradually grew larger and larger. I had plenty of time to think, to observe my new home and to slip into its routine.

Bao Ruo-wang (Jean Pasqualini) and Rudolph Chelminski, *Prisoner of Mao,* (G.P. Putnam's Sons; Coward, McCann & Geoghegan, Inc.), pp. 36-43.

Quotations of Chairman Mao

To overthrow this feudal power is the real objective of the national revolution. What Dr. Sun Yat-sen wanted to do in forty years he devoted to the national revolution but failed to accomplish, the peasants have accomplished in a few months. This is a marvelous feat which has never been achieved in the last forty or even thousands of years. It is a very good thing indeed. It is not a "mess" at all. It is anything but "an awful mess."

As to who is bad and who is not, who is the most ruthless and who is less so, and who is to be severely punished and who is to be dealt with lightly, the peasants keep perfectly clear accounts and very seldom has there been any discrepancy between the punishment and the crime.

A revolution is not the same as inviting people to dinner, or writing an essay, or painting a picture, or doing fancy needlework; it cannot be anything so refined, so calm and gentle, or so mild, kind, courteous, restrained, and magnanimous. A revolution is an uprising, an act of violence whereby one class overthrows another . . . To put it bluntly, it was necessary to bring about a brief reign of terror in every rural area; otherwise one could never suppress the activities of the counterrevolutionaries in the countryside or overthrow the authorities of the gentry. To right a wrong it is necessary to exceed the proper limits, and the wrong cannot be righted without the proper limits being exceeded.

The Chinese nation is not only famous throughout the world for its stamina and industriousness, but also as a freedom-loving people with a rich revolutionary tradition. The history of the Hans, for instance, shows that the Chinese people would never submit to rule by the dark forces and that in every case they succeeded in overthrowing or changing such a rule by revolutionary means. In thousands of years of the history of the Hans, there have been hundreds of insurrections, great or small, against the regime of darkness imposed by the landlords and nobility . . . However, since neither new productive forces, nor new relations of production, nor a new class force, nor an advanced political party existed in those days, and consequently peasant uprisings and wars lacked correct leadership as is given by the proletariat and the Communist Party today, the peasant revolutions invariably failed, and the peasants were utilized during or after each revolution by the landlords and the nobility as a tool for bringing about a dynastic change. Thus, although some social progress was made after each great peasant revolutionary struggle, the feudal economic regulations and feudal political system remainéd basically unchanged.

"You are autocrats." My dear Sirs, you are right, that is just what we are. All the experience the Chinese people have accumulated through several decades teaches us to enforce the people's democratic dictatorship – which one could also call people's democratic autocracy, the two terms mean the same thing – that is, to deprive the reactionaries of the right to speak and let the people alone have that right.

10

The Continuing Revolution

"The tree may prefer calm, but the wind will not subside."
– an old Chinese saying which is one of Mao's favorites.

In spite of their obvious losses of time, material and, most of all, prestige, in the Great Leap Forward, the Communists kept control. They slowed down and dug in. Slowly the economy revived, the communes were reinstated in some places, and the people recovered their energy and good will. Once again, agriculture regained first priority, and gradually the harvests improved and the people's welfare recovered again. Mao's overconfidence in assuming that a nation can industrialize overnight had been discredited. It was the frenzy created by his speed and over-enthusiasm which in some respects had undermined the Great Leap Forward. He had really been proved as naive as all the non-Chinese world leaders described him. Did the man know what he was doing?

Yet he clung to his office and the people didn't desert him. As he grew older, they affectionately emphasized his role in Chinese history by calling him the Great Helmsman. His leadership secured, Mao clung to his style and even intensified it. Mao's style was to advocate two things at once, with no one but Mao knowing which per cent of his support was going to one, which per cent to the other, at any given moment in time. His use of dialectical reasoning was much like the Taoists' use of paradox. To learn about a given object or problem, he examined its opposites, and pitted one against the other, thus learning more and more until he saw it whole. This was an approved Marxist-Leninist mode of reasoning, one which allowed a change of mind often without seeming scatterbrained or unprincipled. Mao used it to the same purpose.

Mao's dialectical reasoning reinforced the old red/expert dichotomy with other contrasts. It became obvious after the Great Leap Forward that there were other areas in which the Communist Party had at least two demonstrated policies operating at the same time. Mao liked it that way, and felt that it kept the people awake, the air clear and yeasty, and the leaders from becoming too stodgy and opinionated.

The questions still open during the early 1960's concerned leadership – should Mao be the charismatic inspirer or the careful planner? They concerned the economy – should it be based on agriculture or on industry, on the countryside or on the city? They concerned the perfect Communist – should he be educated, methodical, cautious, or should he operate on risk and instinct? Should he be more reliant on thought or on action? Should or should not China accept Russia as an ally and example? Did Mao want China to re-emerge into the world as an equal, developed, serious modern state, or did he want to remain xenophobic, isolated, doing his little wonders behind what came to be called a "bamboo curtain"?

During the early 1960's, as China was recovering both from the Great Leap Forward and from the sudden removal of Soviet advisors and materiel in 1960, no clear party line was emerging on these issues. In that vacuum, it is now believed, the Chinese may have withdrawn slightly from the vast attempts at socialism which were made in the 1950's. The collectives and the people's basic loyalty to the regime were not in question, but the communes were held up, the Party's plans were in a holding pattern, and in any transitional state, failure to go forward is simply failure. Besides, bureaucratic red tape and what Mao called "commandism" have a way of reappearing unless they are specifically beaten off. If one isn't vigilant, Mao knew, those in command will begin to think that they are actually a little smarter, a little more energetic, even a little better than the rest of the people. They will accept hierarchy and elitism as natural products of social grouping, just as Confucius did. They will expect higher salaries, job security, more opportunities for their children, and the ability to make what they consider wise decisions themselves, without reference to the party line.

In spite of all the precautions against this thinking, all the thought reform, all the self-criticism built into the Party's "struggle meetings," and all the care which had been taken to pick people who were ideologically "sound" and of a "reliable" class background, the Party was running into "commandism" again by the mid-sixties. Although the people seemed confident, many cadres were beginning to wonder whether Mao's impulsive, "storm the opposition" techniques would actually work in bringing about economic development. Fear of short-lived ideological campaigns and of Mao's admitted desire for a "permanent revolution" had led the cadres to be cautious, less energetic, even less enthusiastic. Even the Red Army was falling back into the hierarchic ways that armies tend to feel are necessary. There were ranks again, differential pay, and uniforms – a far cry from the Long March!

Although Mao had ostensibly retired from administration, he was determined that the aim of socialization should never be abandoned. When he looked at Russia, he saw what he called "revisionists" everywhere, people who had lost sight of the original egalitarian mission, and who had settled into a comfortable, fixed, hierarchic state. He did *not* want that to happen in China, yet when he sent out orders to the Party cadres to "rectify commandism" where he saw it, they never quite got around to it.

As Mao grew older he determined to make his point at least once more. The first step was to re-politicize the People's Liberation Army, under its new leader, Lin Piao, who had been with Mao on the Long March, and who was willing to criticize Russian military methods, renounce modern warfare's emphasis on technology, and return to the basic guerrilla strategy. Many new recruits and a more persistent Party presence within each company made sure that Mao's ideas would be heard. Military ranks were again abandoned and the army mixed with the people more, doing good deeds, acting as a benevolent presence. Finally, the army was held up before the rest of the people as a responsible institution that had been able to "democratize itself."

If the army, why not the Party? This proved more difficult than the army had been. Mao's directives to Liu Shao-ch'i, who had been designated his successor, were not executed quickly or in good spirit. Thus it was that during 1965 there were many mass meetings and parades in an effort to generate support from *outside* the Communist Party. Groups of youth, called the Red Guard, were brought together forcibly by Mao to remind the Party of its roots. Taking Mao's words on "commandism," "revisionism" and "bourgeois traits" as guidelines, they tried to point out to the people at the local level just what their mistakes had been. There was much excitement, fear, and often a lack of control over these numerous "struggle meetings." Hundreds of Party members knuckled under the strain and were sent away, "purged" from the Party. Although they were not imprisoned, their careers had been damaged, perhaps beyond repair. Many young people escaped to Hong Kong, where their main complaint about Communist China was of unfulfilled personal expectations.

Others went to what were called "May 7 Schools" for "rectification and re-education." This combined physical labor with many hours of thought reform. In a variation of the "hsia fang" movement, men and women whose work had always kept them in the universities or in high level jobs in the cities now found themselves in the countryside. A sixty-year-old professor of metallurgy worked in a mine. A high-level economist brought in the crops. Returning to Peking – anything from six months to several years later – they raved about the experience as illuminating, cleansing, and an education which books could never have provided.

It was a very anti-intellectual period. The universities were nearly all closed down. Where educational decisions were being made, young men and women were chosen for further study, not on the basis of their academic promise, but on the basis of their political consciousness. Much emphasis was placed on one's sociological position, for if you were the child of middle-class parents, you would have very little chance to prepare yourself for a demanding or a prestigious job. On the other hand, the children of poor peasants had advantages, no matter how well or poorly they had been doing in school. The society's totem pole was almost completely inverted, with the poor child enjoying greater expectations than his middle-class counterpart.

As the movement continued in 1966 and 1967, many of the teenagers were trained in Peking to rout out what were called the "Four Olds," old ideology, old thought, old habits and old customs. Then they were sent back home on their own Long March, copies of the "Little Red Book" *(Quotations from Chairman Mao Tse-tung)* in their hands, to be used in judgment, accusation, and government. In spite of the chaos of the times, they could not help but remind one of the traditional Chinese scholar, preparing to rule with nothing but his moral uprightness for support.

Again, the stress was on "redness;" to each according to his need; less reverence for technology; more control over artists and writers, ensuring that their contributions were helpful and enthusiastic; a severely restricted group of cultural offerings, firmly coordinated by the new cultural leader, Mao's wife, the former actress Chiang Ching; a big build-up of the "cult of Mao," with shrines constructed wherever he had lived; withdrawal from a complex modern economy; renunciation of western medicine, and glorification instead of the "barefoot doctors" and their ancient remedies; less security for the leaders of any given collective; more "guidance from the masses." Mao wanted revolutionary committees set up which would infuse local governments with the Red Guard and the People's Liberation Army spirit. As local conflicts grew violent, the army had to be called in more and more to keep order. By the end of 1968, Mao had turned on Liu Shao-ch'i and on Teng Hsaio-p'ing, Liu's knowledgeable assistant, calling them too right-wing and too reliant on experts, and had them removed from the Party. Liu's replacement, and now Mao's successor, was to be Lin Piao, which reflected both Mao's personal confidence in him and the vastly increased power of the P.L.A. (People's Liberation Army).

School Play Demonstrating Acupuncture

The movement, however, had spun its course, as such frenzy cannot last. After 1968 the riots and violence ceased, on Mao's orders. The universities gradually re-opened, some of the Party cadres were restored to favor and influence, and the Party was rebuilt. One might say that the Great Cultural Revolution was over, but China's troubles were not. Only slowly did her economy recover from the extensive disruptions of 1965-1968. The leadership of valuable men such as Chou En-lai had been muted. The younger generation had grown weary with Mao's apparently frantic obsession with power; they were bored with the long meetings and discouraged at the small number of "acceptable" movies and plays.

By 1972 Mao was suspicious of the leadership again. Whereas Liu Shao-ch'i had been considered too "right-wing," now Lin Piao was considered too "left-wing." By trying to push the revolution too far, it was argued, he was jeopardizing it. Nor was he patient enough in waiting for his true Chairmanship to begin. As Chou En-lai put it, talking with western newsmen: "Although Lin Piao had become the successor at the Ninth Congress, his mind was not at ease. He knew that he could not really become the successor (until Mao died) . . ."*

The P.L.A. had been told that its role as a central institution in the state would be only temporary. It was told to help to rebuild the Party, which would then return to its former dominance in the decision-making process. This was a policy understandably hard for the army to accept. They knew, moreover, that however easy Mao might find it to criticize "Rightism," that in criticizing "Leftism" he was weakening his own position. Finally, as they watched Mao grow frailer every year, they wondered how long he would live.

Because of these considerations, many of the army officers who had been put into important positions after the Cultural Revolution held on tight when Mao began to criticize their approach. Not only that, but in some cases they actually resisted Mao's policies. They could get away with this, as Mao well knew (having used the same technique himself during his Changsha days) because of the dialectical approach which the Marxists-Leninists-Maoists favored. If criticized for any policy, one can always find a precedent for it or even statements favoring it in the Chairman's own writings. Thus the Party simmered from 1969 until 1971.

In 1972 the whole confrontation came out into the open. Chinese leaders accused Lin Piao and others of trying to overthrow the government, and even of planning to kill Mao himself. The plot had been discovered, the authorities claimed, in September, 1971, on a train speeding southwards from Peking. Frantic, Lin Piao fled the train and got hold of a plane in which he tried to defect to Russia, but it took off in such haste that adequate supplies were not loaded. At any rate, for some reason it crashed in Mongolia, killing and burning beyond recognition all who were

*Philip Bridgham, "The Fall of Lin Piao", in *The China Quarterly,* 55, (July/September 1973), p. 429.

on board. The Chinese claimed to know that Lin Piao was among them because of dental records, but the Russians replied that *their* searches indicated that no one of Lin's age was on board. After this incident, (whose description is still questioned by foreign observers but is apparently accepted in China) Lin Piao and his followers were all denounced as traitors in the Chinese press. China's relationship with Russia was especially tense at that time. They were nearly at war over several issues, and this "defection" didn't help matters at all.

Once again, Mao regained control by identifying certain "enemies of the people." These few people were accused of a litany of crimes, everything from being "swindlers" to becoming a "tool in restoring capitalism," quite a trick for a Left Deviationist. But by now Mao's word made it so.

After Lin Piao's death, Mao retreated more and more to his country house in Hunan province, and ostensibly a collective leadership took over China. This was obviously to protect any single leader from Mao's increasing paranoia. The army was returned to its old position as the "servant of politics." Several former Party workers who had been retired at the time of the Great Cultural Revolution were brought again into favor.

One of the most noteworthy of these was Liu Shao-ch'i's old comrade, Teng Hsiao-p'ing, who was recalled from the oblivion of house arrest in Peking. Well known as a pragmatist, Teng had even been heard to say that "It doesn't matter whether a cat is black or white, so long as it catches mice." What a statement in ideological modern China! A fierce advocate of industrialization and modernization for China, Teng believed in reliance on experts, even if this led to the danger of inequality or even "commandism." Mao could not be expected to be very enthusiastic about Teng's ideas – or vice versa.

Nevertheless, Teng and others who felt as he did were restored to favor in order to help China's emergence as a full-fledged state into the modern world. In mid-1971, Henry Kissinger, the United States Secretary of State, was invited to China, and in early 1972 President Richard M. Nixon made a visit. It must be admitted that President Nixon was received with great courtesy, even if suspicion persists that the Chinese considered it a "tribute-bearing" mission. Although the Chinese have continued some clandestine activities in Southeast Asia and Africa, on the whole China's diplomatic relationships have come out in the open and have been less militant than at various periods in the 1950's and 1960's.

Chou En-lai

China's restraint when the United States was bombing Vietnam and Cambodia can only be called remarkable. She has joined the United Nations, where she has proven a serious and responsible member. It was to set up that mission to the U.N. that Teng Hsaio-p'ing was brought back into power.

The new policy of internationalism was that of Chou En-lai, China's intelligent and cosmopolitan number two (through ten!), man to Mao ever since the Ching Kang Shan days. For the strength of his commitment to the new China, for sheer lasting power in a chaotic time and place, and for his relationship with the turbulent Mao, Chou has been an extraordinary figure in modern Chinese history. During the period of what was called the "Second Cultural Revolution" in early 1974, which seemed to be flogging dead horses like Lin Piao, Confucius and Beethoven,* "China watchers," reading between the lines, concluded that Chou was being threatened. However, since he presented no succession problem (being nearly as old and sick as Mao himself), and since Mao supported his policy of opening China more to the West, he survived this danger as he had survived all the others. The "Second Cultural Revolution" sputtered and died.

Scene in a Day Nursery.

One might ask why Mao supported Chou's policy even as weakly as he did. The answer will not be clear for a while, but it seems that Mao's biggest concern, even during the Vietnam War, was with the menace of Russia. The enemy he had known well seemed more dangerous to him than the enemy he knew only slightly. There was, of course, the common frontier, and the tangible memory of Russian domination from the tsars to the Comintern to Khrushchev. Fellow Communists, moreover, seemed to have even more to argue about than Communists and capitalists. Mao's position as leader of China was secure. It now remained to see who, or whose ideas, would control the world Communist movement.

*Confucius was a code-word for the acceptance of hierarchy and experts; Beethoven for the acceptability of foreign contact.

As soon as China was "open," American visitors flocked in, happy to follow the routes prescribed for them by China's tourist bureau. They marveled at the clean streets, at the factories which had been built, at the fact that there were no longer any beggars or prostitutes in Shanghai. Most of all they reported the genuine enthusiasm which ordinary people seemed to feel about the "liberation," the Party and Mao himself. Such different observers as Professor John K. Fairbank, Republican Senator Hugh Scott, and columnist Ann Landers came back impressed. Mao seemed to have the modern Chinese version of "the mandate." His ideological flexibility, his ability to increase productivity, his talents and passionate convictions, but most of all the universal feeling that he loved the people, made his hold both tight and gentle – a perfect Chinese ruler.

Still, the world held its breath in the mid-seventies, when it seemed that Mao was near death. Even the most casual western observer, to say nothing of the 800 million Chinese, wondered what would happen to the nation and the revolution after Mao was no longer on the scene.

Going to the Countryside

Recently, large numbers of educated youths in many cities have rushed to the countryside, forming a new revolutionary current. This is an indication of prosperity of our nation, and a symbol of unceasing development in education in our country. Going to rural and mountainous areas, urban educated youths have embarked upon a glorious revolutionary road – a road on which they can join the masses of workers and peasants.

Some urban educated youths may ask: What can we do in rural and mountainous areas? Is there a bright future in plowing the soil? Our reply is: Educated youths will have an endless, bright and great future in rural and mountainous areas.

Why do we say so?

In the eyes of a proletarian, the future of a revolutionary is always closely linked with the future of the revolutionary cause. Our country's agriculture has extensive prospects, and our country's five hundred million peasants have a great future . . .

Educated youths in some cities say: "Rural life is hard!" Yes, this is true. Though agricultural construction is now much better than that before the liberation, the laboring conditions are still poorer and life is harder in the countryside than in urban areas. Going suddenly to the countryside, we may not be accustomed to the environment physically and technically and in everyday life. Only if we make up our minds to temper ourselves, shall we be able, after a certain period of time, to get accustomed to the rural environment. If we think that what hardships we suffer today are for the sake of building a new, socialist countryside, creating happiness for the younger generation, and rendering greater support to the revolutionary struggles undertaken by peoples of the world, we shall find happiness in rural life and shall not feel any suffering. It is good for youths to suffer some hardships during their time of growth. A revolutionary youth fears no hardships, does not wish to pass his days in quietness and comfort, but wishes to lead a life of fierce struggle. He is willing to create the world with his hands, instead of waiting to enjoy other people's achievements. The harder the conditions are, the more can he temper his revolutionary character and perseverance and learn the skills of overcoming difficulties. Many educated youths who have gone to the countryside have realized that it is impossible to carry out revolution and change the backward aspects of the countryside without first suffering some hardships and shedding blood and sweat. When they had just started to labor, blisters were formed on their hands, and their shoulders swelled as a result of carrying heavy loads. However, they were not scared by these difficulties. They said: "If we do not suffer hardships, we can never temper ourselves." "Suffering of hardships helps us get rid of arrogance and establish a revolutionary will." Imposing demands on themselves in this spirit, they will fear no hardships or tiring work, and can overcome all sorts of difficulties.

It can be easily understood that youths show concern for their future. The Party and the state also hope that the youths will have a beautiful and bright future. The purpose of carrying out the revolution and national reconstruction is to enable the people of the whole country and the younger generation to have a beautiful and bright future. Since we go to rural and mountainous areas for the purpose of carrying out revolution, we must, while considering problems concerning our future, combine our individual prospects with the great socialist cause. We must dedicate our wisdom and strength to the service of the motherland and the people and, by the effort of this generation, build a socialist new countryside. Educated-youth comrades, go bravely to the agricultural front, and let us press ahead bravely on the road of revolutionization! . . .

Franz Schurmann and Orville Schell, *The China Reader: Communist China*, (Random House, 1967), pp. 456-7.

A Westerner is Impressed

FANCHENG, China, May 19 — Five gray cars with horns rasping drove right onto the platform of the railroad station here early today to pick up the first foreigners to visit this area deep in the Chinese interior in more than 20 years.

A group of district and municipal dignitaries headed by two vice chairmen of the regional Revolutionary Committee were gathered at the station along with masses of intensely curious people.

It was 7:30 A.M., but we – my father, Chester A. Ronning, my sister Sylvia and I – had been up since sunrise looking out through the train windows.

We had traveled by plane the 550 miles south-southwestward

from Peking to Wuhan and all night by train the 175 miles north-westward from there. The hilly green, plush countryside here in Hupeh Province was a welcome contrast to the flat fields in the Peking area.

Chester Ronning, who was born here in 1894, spent his first 13 years in this area and later taught in the school his father had founded. He was welcomed home as a native, a "lump of mud," as people here often modestly call themselves.

He spent the years from 1945 to 1951 as charge d'affaires of the Canadian Embassy in Chungking and Nanking, but this was his first visit to his birthplace since 1927. He was amazed by the changes.

"In those days," he said, "the villages were clusters of mudhuts surrounded by high mud walls. Every village had a watchtower and guards on constant surveillance against bands of robbers and soldiers who would loot and rob the villages."

Now the watchtowers are gone and most of the houses are of brick.

Our cavalcade of honking cars drove over a bridge across the River Han to Fancheng's twin city of Siangyang.

We had expected to rough it in the interior of China, so we were amazed to arrive at a very good guest house. It had been built in 1966 and the interior was freshly whitewashed. It is also used for meetings of the revolutionary committee.

The rooms were comfortably furnished with bamboo furniture and double beds with embroidered satin quilts and pillow cases.

Four smiling girls in white jackets were assigned to bring us all the hot water we could use. They did their job so well that every time we came in we were ushered to the bathtub.

After breakfast, we went sightseeing – first a walk on the city wall.

With a thousand eyes watching us we climbed to the drum-and-bell-tower on top of an old pavilion where, as Father explained to our Chinese guides in fluent Chinese, scholars used to retire for study.

When the guide said the broken bronze bell on top had been used to tell the time, Father interrupted him, to the amusement of our Chinese friends.

"The bell was not used for telling time," he said, "but for ceremonial purposes. The time was given by a man called a ta-ken-ti who would walk through the streets sounding a gong and singing out the time."

The ta-ken-ti also beat a night song to warn of thieves, he explained.

The Chinese soon gave up trying to show us around and urged Father to take over.

We visited the north gate at Siangyang and looked across the river to Fancheng. From there we could see the house in the old Lutheran mission compound where Father had lived. His parents, Halvor and Hannah Ronning, were among the first Lutheran missionaries to come to China. She died here in 1907.

Father recalled how the people in Fancheng and Siangyang lived in terror of the fierce Han River. During flood periods both cities were often submerged. In 1938 more than 3,000 people were drowned in a flood. Even as late as 1960 and 1964, the area suffered from flooding.

In 1964, however, the people turned out to widen and strengthen the dikes. Now with 26 miles of sturdy embankments along both sides, the river is contained. The water can rise five or six feet above the former danger level without flooding.

In the afternoon, we paid a visit to a rural commune, and in the evening we were invited to a banquet given by the chairman of the revolutionary committee. It was a multicourse dinner, including wild chicken, rabbit, fish eggs and a delicious monkey-head mushroom soup.

Ho Fung-wu, a vice chairman of the Revolutionary Committee, explained that the population, which was 40,000 "before the liberation," had risen to 189,000. This is mostly a result of new industry.

"Before the liberation," he said, "there was no modern industry in this area. We had a machine repair shop with 21 workers, four handicraft shops, a cigarette rolling shop and over 100 blacksmiths. Now we have transformed a consumer city into a productive one."

He said that 106 of the 200 large and small factories now here had been built during the campaign of the late nineteen-fifties for rapid industrialization that was known as the Great Leap Forward.

In a discussion of education and culture, it was pointed out that my grandfather founded the first modern school here in 1893 and when Father returned as a lecturer in 1922 there were only three middle – or junior high – schools with a total of 1,500 students. Now there are 38 middle schools with 13,000 students.

When asked about the average income, Mr. Ho said it was comparatively low as a result of an influx of new workers into the area.

He said that there was no unemployment and that there was still a need of more manpower.

"Mr. Ronning knows better than I do what it was like here 44 years ago," Mr. Ho said. "He can also see our shortcomings. He knows, for instance, that we must raise our standard of mechanization of agriculture and raise our potential to fight against natural catastrophes. Last year our cotton yield dropped and there are still many unpaved roads and highways.

"The work on our buildings is not fast enough. We have a long way to go."

Father replied: "When I was a child here, many of the people did not even have a roof over their heads. Only the merchants, officials and landlords had adequate housing.

"Today, on our trip, I saw many new houses. They are not so big or elaborate, but they are adequate and clean."

"The changes in Hupeh Province," he remarked, "are beyond my expectations. If there were no Chinese on the landscape, I would almost think it was a foreign country."

From the New York Times *Report from Red China,* (New York, 1972), pp. 148-151.

11

Death of the
Great Helmsmen

In the middle of the 1970's, Mao and Chou once again asserted their control over Chinese politics, but it was the control of two old men. It was obvious that Mao was getting more and more senile, being unable to speak clearly and, toward the end, unable to follow conversations. He was rarely seen in the capital, being in retirement in Hunan. Chou was in Peking, as lucid as ever, but he too was less available for consultation, and his interviews, when they were given, took place in the hospital. His face, rarely photographed, took on the look of one who was struggling with cancer.

The shrewd and knowledgeable Teng Hsiao-p'ing was brought back from the U.N. and given more and more of Chou's tasks, particularly those of talking to important western visitors. It became clear that he was Chou's chosen heir-apparent. Teng believed in the moderate, internationalist approach favored by Chou, though he could hardly be said to have Chou's charm and flexibility, nor his willingness to play a number-two position.

Mao's relationship with his wife, Chiang Ching, deteriorated during his last years. As a strong spokesman for the radical faction during the Great Cultural Revolution, she was able to exercise much control over which movies were shown, which books were published, and which views of Mao were revealed to the public. Much younger than Mao, she had her own friends, especially Wang Hung-wen, a young Shanghai union leader who had also gained prominence in the Great Cultural Revolution, becoming vice president of the Party. Other friends included Chang Chun-chiao, deputy secretary of the Shanghai Municipal Committee, who had become Deputy Prime Minister, and Yao Wen-yuan, the editor-in-chief of the Shanghai Liberation Daily. These were all ardent Communists of the more red, "frankly-left" persuasion. Believers in pure communism, they were against putting much emphasis on industrialization, against privileges for inventors or managers or even wage increases for the workers. They have, however, been accused of not having any real program, radical or moderate – of not, in fact, believing in anything except their own

Tien An Men Square

power. Chiang Ching used her new prominence and her position as Mao's wife to promote the welfare of these men. They came to be called the "Gang of Four," although there were more than four in their faction.

Although it was not widely known at the time, Mao grew tired of her dictatorial methods, and even slightly afraid of her zeal, in spite of the fact that it was modeled so closely after his own. As early as July 1966 he was said to have written an open letter to her in which he said: "I think you had better pay more attention to this problem, don't let success make you dizzy. One must frequently give thought to one's own weaknesses, shortcomings, and mistakes. I don't know how many times I've discussed this point with you. It was only in April in Shanghai that we talked about it."*

That settled things for then, but as he grew weaker she grew stronger, and he grew more wary of her strength. Finally he felt that they should separate, and meet only by appointment, so that she would not use her position by his bedside to decide who would be his visitors and what would be his policies. He criticized her in public, and at least once disassociated himself from what she was saying. He criticized her Shanghai friends, too, and it is said that it was he who originally used the term "Gang of Four" in advising them not to form factions.

When Chou En-lai died in January of 1976, there was an unexpected outpouring of grief for him, and it became apparent that he had been a more important folk hero to the Chinese people than most China watchers had realized. In Tien An Men Square there was actually a confrontation between thousands of people who wanted to pile wreaths on Chou's monument and the authorities, who had been ordered to take them away. This battle on Peking's streets was spontaneous, reflecting feelings which have been acknowledged more fully since, but it was also the first view of an important schism in Chinese leadership. The tensions between the moderates, led by Teng, and the radicals, led by the Gang of Four, erupted publically. Within a few months, Teng Hsiao-p'ing had been accused of being a "capitalist-roader" and retired again. A newcomer, Hua Kuo-feng, a sturdy, relatively unknown governor of Mao's own province, Hunan, emerged as Mao's choice to lead China. He looked like a relatively unambitious, unsophisticated moderate, a good participant in a collectivist leadership, a good transition figure.

*Hsin Chi, "The Rise and Fall of the 'Gang of Four'", (Books New China, Inc., New York, 1977), p. 19.

He was unknown in ideology or style to either the western observers or to most of China. Besides that, we now know that he was more and more distrustful of Chiang Ching and her colleagues, who seemed to represent the city whereas he represented the countryside, thus confusing the usual stereotypes of reds and experts. The Gang of Four seemed to grow more and more dominant during the spring of 1976 and their power obviously threatened Hua's position. The faltering Chinese economy, the massive earthquakes in June (Heaven's signs?), and threats of floods in the Yellow River basin also added to his problems. He handled them, however, in a forthright and effective manner which increased Mao's confidence, and Chinese confidence generally, in his leadership. Mao evidently wrote a note to Hua during this period which said, "With you in charge, I'm at ease," a modern version of the Imperial Seal, and one which Hua has had widely reproduced.

When Mao died in September, Hua determined that he must immediately confront the Gang of Four. Chiang Ching, as the widow, was given a central place in the ceremonies, but they were run by Hua. The first inkling of trouble for the Four came in the eulogy itself, when Hua was describing what Mao had wanted for China. In the speech prepared for him, which was written partly by the Gang of Four, it was distinctly written that among Mao's last words had been the advice: "Act according to the principles laid down." Stating this as an official directive would have strengthened Chiang Ching considerably, because it would have emphasized the revolutionary and romantic rather than the practical and material nature of Mao's contribution. But Hua did not read the phrase, and observers noticed that Wang Hung-wen, standing just behind Hua, seemed to grow more and more nervous, and finally craned his head so that he could catch sight of the words in Hua's speech. In the next few weeks the official attack on the Gang of Four began. In the newspapers and in single-character posters put up in all the major cities, the Gang was accused of being too idealistic, impractical, and callous to the needs of the people. They were even accused of putting the revolution in danger by their abuse of power.

Many new stories have surfaced since then about the antagonistic and arrogant methods of the Gang of Four, their pettiness, their "adventurism" and their neglect of China's material needs. Chiang Ching, who had always maintained a rather serious, drab image, has now been accused of wanting to set herself up as another Empress, wearing western clothes and watching western movies on the sly, offering her daughter's hand in marriage to a political ally, and

提高警惕

Young People in China

even of too great a reliance on silk sheets for her bed.

Except for a stormy trial in the fall of 1980, the Gang of Four have not been seen in public since their arrest. Hua's campaign against them, however, has been far from easy to accomplish. The Chinese economy had been insidiously affected both by the uncertainty symbolized by their leadership and their own philosophy, which, reputedly, can be summarized in their statement, "We would rather have a socialist train late than a capitalist train on time." It has now been revealed that in Chinese industry during Mao's last years there had been a multitude of lost workdays, card parties right in the factories, and, of course, late trains.

Hua claims that the Gang of Four attempted a coup, and that his move against them was really a counter-coup. This hasn't been proved, but it is true that Hua's action seems to have been popular with the majority of the Chinese. One western journalist reported soon after Chiang Ching's fall that when he had been in a Peking theatre the year before, and one of her films came on the screen, there was a chorus of booing and more than half of the audience got up and stalked out. She was certainly unpopular, perhaps reminding many Chinese of another Empress Dowager.

There have, nevertheless, been pockets of resistance to the government's actions, especially in the Fukien and Szechwan provinces, and there was much vandalism and unrest in late 1976 and early 1977. More single character posters were put up to explain the new mass line. Armies were sent to areas resisting the government in this newest campaign. Mao was given what a *New York Times* reporter, Fox Butterfield, calls an "unofficial posthumous divorce" from Chiang Ching, and the regime has been busily publishing all Mao's reservations about her character. In fact, much is now made of his first wife, who was executed by the Nationalists in 1930.* Pictures of her are appearing in the press, and where Chiang Ching once stood in certain old well-known photos, there is now only a blacked-out shadow.

By the summer of 1977, Hua felt ready to move beyond mere resistance to his political rivals and into the development of new policies for China. Although he was persistently described as a "leftist," especially since he had been put into power by Mao himself, he authorized a movement toward industrialization, modernization and greater contacts with foreigners, all of which were considered "rightist" policies.

One of the most knowledgeable and forceful advocates of these new policies, Teng Hsiao-p'ing, was still under house arrest, but Hua allowed him to be officially "rehabilitated," and to emerge for the third time as one of China's major leaders. Whether Hua was forced to do this by Teng's allies or whether he felt he personally needed Teng is unclear. At any rate, Teng's position as Vice Chairman of the Party has masked only slightly the fact that he is the real ruler of China. Although Hua held on to his position as Chairman until June of 1981, and although he was then made one of its Vice Chairmen, the policies and the political leaders of post-Mao China have been sharply different from those in the ten years before Mao's death.

For a brief period, Teng even seemed to experiment with allowing greater freedom of expression than had been seen in a long time. People were allowed to put up posters, letters, and petitions, all avidly recorded by the expanded Western press, on what was called "democracy wall" in Peking. After a few weeks, however, Teng

Teng Hsiao-p'ing

seemed to lose his nerve, and the police once again prevented any activities around the wall.

The biggest changes since Mao's death were made in the economy. The leaders in the government, who seem delighted to be called pragmatists, proceeded with an ambitious program of construction, development of resources, upgrading of the army, and increases in their contacts with the West. Although Westerners were realizing by the spring of 1981 that China would not be able to pay for all the ambitious plans being made, much has nevertheless been done in a short time.

While this is clearly "deMaoification," it is still not labelled as such in the Chinese press. At the sixtieth anniversary of the founding of the Chinese Communist Party, in July of 1981, China's leaders offered an assessment of Mao's leadership. In a long explanation, they said that Mao was an inspired and effective revolutionary and that before 1949 all challenges to his powers and his ideology were incorrect and dangerous. However, after about 1957, they asserted, Mao became increasingly isolated and capricious. He acted both arbitrarily and "arrogantly" and became too full of his own special vision. The last ten years of his life, all labelled the "Cultural Revolution" in this communique, were therefore described as especially harmful for China.

Thus the record is a mixed one, and China's real enemies are seen to be those who exploited Mao, such as the Gang of Four, rather than Mao himself. His tomb in Peking is still mobbed with visitors, both foreign and Chinese. Mao's most romantic and "frankly-left" policies are being abandoned, but there is not the attempt, as there was in Russia after Stalin, totally to discredit the leader as well as his policies.

The current stress on non-ideological matters does not mean that the present leaders of China are not Communists. The commune as a political form is flourishing, and government control over the economy and over the lives of the people seems as strong as ever. In the summer of 1980, for example, the government issued strong directives designed to keep couples from having more than one child. This was a clear assertion of national power and responsibility over decisions which were once kept in the family.

There is little doubt that a vast rise in the average person's standard of living has been accomplished since 1949 under the Communists. More contacts with the West only reveal more gaps between China and her modern ideal; this reinforces, in many Chinese minds, the need for a vigorous and authoritarian government; and China's present leadership, policies and totalitarian approach seem to be without serious resistance.

Teng's pragmatic and internationalist policies find favor in the Western press, yet Westerners tend to feel that there are still serious problems in China. Although the trial of the Gang of Four ended with jail sentences instead of death and other harsh punishments from the Chinese past, the legal methods and attitudes which were partly revealed to the Chinese and to the world public were not as protective of individual rights as the Chinese claimed. Another difficult problem remains that of succession. There are still no commonly accepted procedures for the transfer of power, for who will decide on it and on what basis. Having been on the Long March can no longer be considered a prime prerequisite, but what will take its place? These questions inevitably lead to much speculation (inside and outside China) and a constant jockeying for position which makes Chinese politics highly unstable. A third problem, at least from the Western point of view, is what Barbara Tuchman has termed the "mental monotone" in Chinese political and intellectual life, the expected conformity in writings, speech, and behavior. Time will tell whether these disadvantages are necessary trade-offs to the rise in Chinese power and plenty which has been evident since 1949.

The Sino-American relationship improved in December 1978 when President Carter announced that the United States was prepared to recognize the People's Republic of China. This completed "normalization," and meant a change in the American attitude toward the Republic of China on Taiwan, which had claimed to represent China since 1949. How much President Reagan is prepared to withdraw official American political and military support from Taiwan is still uncertain, but as this book went to press, the new administration was even hinting that it might be prepared to supply arms to mainland China.

The improvement in U.S.-China relations over the last ten years has largely depended on the hostility between the United States and Russia, and the deterioration of the Russia-China alliance. During the 1980s, however, as the leadership establishes itself or is replaced, there will be more complexities to add to the earlier and simpler equation. Americans must understand these complexities and be flexible enough to reach accommodation, if they want the present hopeful friendship between these two proud nations to continue and to grow.

BIBLIOGRAPHY

The purpose of any course or book is to open a field to those who may not have dared to venture into it earlier. With that in mind, the documents chosen for this book are not only pieces of writing which augment or illuminate the essay, but are also excerpts from books which it is felt are worth reading in their entirety. All the books cited below have proved to be of interest to students over the years.

In the first category are books which can serve as an overview. The best single-volume example of this kind is *The United States and China* by John K. Fairbank. It describes modern Chinese history, with a special emphasis on where it touches or is touched by the United States. The organization and interpretations of this vast amount of material are distinctive, and reflect Professor Fairbank's brilliance and stature as Dean of American Sinology. The sections on China in *East Asia: The Modern Transformation* were also written by Professor Fairbank, and are somewhat more detailed than *The United States and China*. They could serve as a good reference book for high school students.

Another useful kind of book for beginners in this field is the edited collection. Theodore deBary's *Sources of Chinese Tradition* provides many of the classics of Chinese writing. Franz Schurmann and Orville Schell's collections: *Imperial China, Republican China, Communist China* and *People's China* are well chosen and well introduced, and include writings on China by foreigners as well as Chinese.

Several other books with a more detailed treatment of Chinese history or society have proved to be lively course additions. Arthur Waley's *Three Ways of Thought in Ancient China* presents early Confucianism against the background of its times, but Confucius as a human being is more clearly presented in H.G. Creel's *Confucius and the Chinese Way*. Other stimulating presentations of the Imperial period are Robert Van Gulik's *Judge Dee* mysteries, taken from Chinese sources, very good stories as well as accurate portraits of the times. Jonathan Spence also writes in a style which can be readily appreciated by newcomers to the field, especially in two of his books, *Emperor of China,* collected from the writings of the K'ang Hsi Emperor, and *To Change China: Western Advisers in China 1620-1960,* a series of fascinating essays on those who loved China but at the same time were most concerned with westernizing it. Two of Pearl Buck's books, *The Good Earth* and *Imperial Woman,* have provided good background reading. Books by Lin Yutang and Han Suyin have been useful attempts by Chinese authors to interpret their country for the West. *A Daughter of Han,* which was told by Ning Lao T'ai-t'ai to Ida Pruitt, describes the travails of a poor Chinese woman in the late nineteenth century. Pa Chin's *Family* details the disintegration of the Chinese family a little later, and John Hersey's *A Single Pebble* and Theodore H. White's and Annalee Jacoby's *Thunder Out of China* contribute to this picture of confusion and despair on the modern Chinese scene.

There are many books on Communist China, and more are being written every day, but the following have been most useful and interesting to my students: the books by Edgar Snow, especially *Red Star Over China;* the famous *Fanshen: A Documentary of Revolution in a Chinese Village* by William Hinton, paired with C. K. Yang's *Chinese Communist Society: The Family and The Village;* Jan Myrdal's *Report from a Chinese Village,* and his and Gun Kessle's *China: The Revolution Continued;* and finally *Journey Between Two Chinas,* by Seymour Topping, which provides, from the perspective of a foreigner, a comparison between the China just before "liberation" and that of the early seventies. Modern observers whose work is excellent but which soon may be out of date are Ross Terrill in *800,000,000: The Real China* and *Flowers on an Iron Tree,* and Orville Schell, whose *In the People's Republic* is informative and a delight to read. Fox Butterfield's reports in *The New York Times* are distinguished by his deep study of the field as well as his courage and lively writing.

INDEX

Africa, 29, 36, 69, 170
All Men Are Brothers, 128
Americans, 33, 37, 46, 63, 69, 75, 114, 115, 133, 150
   See also United States.
Amoy, map 53; 59
Annam (North Vietnam), 31
Arrow War, 54-55, 65
Asia, 36, Southeast Asia, 170
Autumn Harvest Rising, 126

Bamboo curtain, 165, 185
Bao Ruo-wang, excerpt, 156-162
Barbarians (Chinese word for foreigners), 35, 39, 40, 42, 44, 46
Beethoven, 172, 172n
Belgian, 74
Blooming Flowers Period, 152
   See also One Hundred Flowers
Boddhisattvas, 30
Bolshevik, 93-94, 125
Border region, 126, 127, 128, 132
Borneo, 31
Boston, 111
Boxers, Order of Righteous and Harmonious Fists, 70, 71
   Boxer Protocol, 71-73
   Boxer Rebellion, 70-73
British, 33, 46, 48, 50, 51, 109
   See also England.
   Arrow War, 54-55
   Boxer Rebellion, 71, 72
   opium trade and war, 35-40
   sphere of influence, 63, 65, 69
   Sun Yat-sen, 75-76
British East India Company, 32, 34
Buck, Pearl, *The Good Earth,* excerpt, 9-11
Buddhism in China, 29-30
Butterfield, Fox, 184

C.C. Brothers, 119
Cambodia, 31, 171
Campaigns, 148, 152, 153
Canton, map XIII; 32, 34, 36, 37, 38, 41, 51, 55, 62

Cantonese, 74, 76, 88, 93, 108, 109, 119, 120, 134
Capitalist-roader, 181
Carter, President, 185
Censors, censorate, 13, 15, 21, 23
Center Country (Middle Kingdom, Chinese name for China), 31, 46
Central Committee, Communist Party, 126, 129
Champa (South Vietnam), 31
Chang Chun-chiao, 179
Chang Hsueh-liang, 112, 114
Chang Tso-lin, 99
Changsha, 126, 169
Chapdelaine, Father, 54
Chekiang, province, map II; 42, 117, 118
Ch'en Chi-mei, 119
Ch'en Tu-hsiu, 93, 125, 126
Chiang Ching, picture 149; 131n, 167, 179, 181, 182, 184
Chiang K'ai-shek, picture 111; 99, 108-116, 124, 126, 129, 131, 133, 134, 136, 139, 141, 150
   description, 117-120
   writings, excerpts from, 121-123
Ch'ien-lung Emperor, 17, 33
   Letter to George III, excerpt from, 41-42
Ch'in dynasty, 12
Chin-shih, status, 19
China Watchers, 172
China's Destiny, 115
   excerpts, 122-123
China's Sorrow, 12. *See also* Yellow River.
Chinese Communist Party, 56, 94, 108, 109, 112, 114, 115
   before 1949, 125-134
   between 1949 and 1961, 145-155
   between 1961 and 1974, 164-173
   between 1974 and 1978, 179-185
Ch'ing dynasty, 16, 48, 51. *See also* Manchus.
Ching Kang Shan mountains, map 127; 126, 128, 129, 171

193